Praise for Dennis Lee

"One of the finest poets in the English language."
— *Quill & Quire*

"Canada has produced many competent poets but few absolute masters. ... *The Gods* confirms the presence of a master: Dennis Lee."
— Mark Abley, *Maclean's*

"The trouble with Dennis Lee's children's rhymes is that they are unforgettable." — Margaret Atwood

"Constantly, throughout his work about intensely personal matters, Lee achieves perhaps the hardest quality for a poet to attain, a memorable directness and simplicity. Which is in turn a token of his preeminence."
— Christopher Levenson, *EVENT*

"Lee, like every great poet, cannot be catalogued or filed under any given poetic category. He is an exponent of the real; his lines are essentially prophetic." — Gwendolyn MacEwen

"Dennis Lee's poems are important to me above all because, more consistently than those of anyone else whose work I know, they manifest a full awareness of the poem as a form of musical score."
— Denise Levertov, *Descant*

"An astonishing batch of poems — unwieldy, tough-minded, shot through with passages of knotty and uncompromising beauty."
— Perry Nodelman, *Winnipeg Free Press*, reviewing *Civil Elegies*

"*Civil Elegies* is our *Waste Land*. ... It gave the city and the nation a sacramental landmark for a secular age." — Nick Mount

"The poems in *Riffs* are honest, passionate and full of insight. Their masterful rhythms and melodies re-establish Lee as one of the country's great poets." — *Montreal Gazette*

"Impossible to put down. Lee has a way of making language seem inevitable. ... Whether the emotional moment swoops or falls, we are taken along for the ride in an entirely convincing, captivating way."
— *Quill & Quire*, reviewing *Riffs*

"Poet Dennis Lee may add love-junkie beatnik of distinction to his long list of credentials." — *NOW Magazine*, reviewing *Riffs*

"*Un* reconfigures English into something as weirdly expressive as it is resistant to paraphrase ... part jazz, part wolf howl, invoking no less than the end of the world." — ROBYN SARAH, *National Post*

"*Un* is a hair-raising yikes of a book. ... There is dread, urgency, anger, nostalgia, and fear, but also a howling love for the world."
— KAREN SOLIE, *Globe and Mail*

"Dennis Lee is the poet laureate of the Canadian kids' world."
— *Montreal Gazette*

"*Yesno* is a masterwork."
— MARK DICKINSON, *Malahat Review*

"This is wild, brave, urgent poetry, not quite like anything else being written; it has no truck with cheap grace or obvious answers, but is a singular, memorable, and necessary book."
— MAGGIE HELWIG, *Globe and Mail*, reviewing *Yesno*

"*Testament* spectacularly channels the inconceivable ... [a] great work."
— *Telegraph Journal*

"The joy of reading *Heart Residence* is reading Lee whole ... How lucky for us as Canadians to have a singer and seer like Dennis Lee."
— J.S. PORTER, *HA&L Magazine*

"One of the most extraordinary bodies of work in contemporary English poetry." — PAUL VERMEERSCH

WRESTLING *with* CADENCE

Books by Dennis Lee

Poetry

Kingdom of Absence, 1967
Civil Elegies, 1968
Civil Elegies and Other Poems, 1972, 2012
The Death of Harold Ladoo [chapbook], 1976
Miscellany [chapbook], 1977
The Gods [chapbook], 1978
The Gods, 1979
Riffs, 1982, 1993, 2015
The Difficulty of Living on Other Planets, 1987
Nightwatch: New and Selected Poems, 1996
Un, 2003
Yesno, 2007
The Bard of the Universe [chapbook], 2007
Testament, 2012
Heart Residence: Collected Poems 1967–2017, 2017

Prose

Savage Fields: An Essay in Literature and Cosmology, 1977
Reading Adonis [chapbook], 1987
Body Music: Essays, 1998
Re-Greening the Undermusic, 2016
Wrestling with Cadence: Essays on Writing and Intuition, 2025

In Translation

Elégies civiles et autres poèmes, 1980
Pasticcio di alligatore e altre poesie, 2002
Ragoût de crocodile, 2005
Dimora del cuore / Heart Residence, 2006

For Children

Wiggle to the Laundromat (Rochdale College), 1967 or 1968
Wiggle to the Laundromat (New Press), 1970
Alligator Pie, 1974
Nicholas Knock and Other People, 1974
Garbage Delight, 1977
The Ordinary Bath, 1979
Jelly Belly, 1983
Lizzy's Lion, 1984
The Dennis Lee Big Book, 1985
The Ice Cream Store, 1991
Ping and Pong, 1993
Dinosaur Dinner, 1997
Bubblegum Delicious, 2000
The Cat and the Wizard, 2001
Garbage Delight: Another Helping, 2002
SoCool, 2004
Alligator Stew, 2005
Melvis and Elvis, 2015
Alligator Pie & Other Poems: A Dennis Lee Treasury, 2020

Anthologies

An Anthology of Verse (with Roberta Charlesworth), 1964, 1989
The Second Century Anthologies of Verse, Book 2 (with Roberta Charlesworth), 1967
The University Game (with Howard Adelman), 1968
T.O. Now: The Young Toronto Poets, 1968
The New Canadian Poets, 1970–1985, 1985

Wrestling *with* Cadence

essays on writing
and intuition

DENNIS LEE

STONEHEWER
BOOKS

ISBN: 978-1-0692362-0-3

1 2 3 4 5 6 7 8 9 10

Cataloguing data available from Library and Archives Canada

Set in Garamond and Bodoni by Ned Seager
Printed and bound by Friesens in Canada

Stonehewer Books | Victoria, BC
stonehewerbooks.com

Stonehewer Books is located on the traditional territory of the Lkwungen people on what is now called Vancouver Island. We acknowledge and are grateful for the unique contributions to our common well-being made by the Indigenous peoples of this land.

This book is dedicated to the memory of Phil Balsam (1943–2023) —
my mentor in songwriting, and my best friend in life.

Contents

Preface

"THIS ISN'T A REPRINT. ... IT'S NOT A MUSEUM. ... IT'S ALMOST a brand new book." That ringing declaration came from George Galt, the cheerfully implacable editor and publisher at Stonehewer Books. He had approached me about doing a memoir, but that wasn't happening any time soon. So we moved on to the essay collection *Body Music*, from 1998. It explored the experience of writing poetry, and it was out of print.

Galt offered the essays a new home. And he pointed out that one topic in particular kept cropping up: something I call *cadence*. But that left him scratching his head — what exactly *was* "cadence"? He couldn't get a bead on it. Would I consider revising the book, with a clearer depiction of cadence as the leitmotif?

I was already itching to recast the essays — to make them more plain-spoken and accessible. So I jumped at the chance. Mind you, I thought Galt was wrong about the depictions of cadence; they were perfectly clear, to me at least. Eventually I realized we were both right; the depictions were clear, and cadence was still a mystery.

Along with the deep-dish revisions, there would be new material. We would retain the essays on Al Purdy and Gaston Miron, as changes of pace. And the title popped up out of nowhere. "Wrestling with cadence" — that's what I'd been doing for decades, and it's what the revised essays would do now. I hoped readers would relish these stories of a tumbling, non-verbal energy, and the intuitive mooching that has sometimes coaxed it into words.

But how to frame the stories?

◆

The essays we've chosen span more than five decades. What holds them together, beyond the concern with cadence? The key is a certain recurring pattern, which you can already see in the earliest piece.

When I began writing poetry seriously, in the early 1960s, my capacity for analytic thinking was miles ahead of my poetic ability. My academic career — in the English Department at the University of Toronto — was flourishing; I became a full-time lecturer while I was doing my M.A. Meanwhile, my progress in poetry was nonexistent. But I could picture the decades to come, stretching out with a kind of burnished inevitability. I would produce a stream of notable literary criticism — and on the side, pen the occasional volume of verse. It was a tempting prospect.

Too tempting, in fact. So in 1967 I resigned, and left the university for keeps. I was twenty-eight, still spinning my wheels as a poet; I couldn't risk staying in the academy any longer. Even though I loved rigorous thinking — no, *because* I loved rigorous thinking — it would be all too easy to go on flexing my intellect, while postponing the claim of poetry indefinitely.

As it turned out, the move released a voice unlike anything I'd written before. Cadence took over. And it happened almost at once — with *Civil Elegies*, a sequence of meditative poems.

That was exhilarating. But I had no idea where the new voice was coming from, or even what it was. So in a talk at a writers' conference, I tried to decipher what had paralyzed my writing for so long, and then blown it wide open. That led to a full-scale essay, "Cadence, Country, Silence."

And this demonstrates what the essays have in common. *Civil Elegies* and "Cadence, Country, Silence" came as a two-pack, with the essay following the poetry. And the same pattern would repeat itself in subsequent decades. My imagination kept switching lanes — exploring one kind of poetry intuitively till I'd done all I could with it, then starting from scratch in a new vein. And periodically I would pause, and try to make sense of what I'd been doing by instinct alone. Usually in an essay — though it might begin as an interview, which I would then recast as an imaginary dialogue.

So these essays and dialogues are the way stations where I stopped, looked back, took stock. And in some cases, they signalled that it was time to become an ignoramus again. Then the familiar cycle would play out once more: intuitive scribbling, followed by retrospective analysis.

Galt's initial proposal, I can see now, was bang on. Almost in spite of myself, I've been composing a slo-mo memoir for half a century. Vignettes from a life in words — and always the undermusic, the cadence.

◆

A few notes may be useful:

- After the first essay, the sequence is chronological. The date and provenance of each piece is given in the "Notes on the Texts" at the end.
- Most of the essays from *Body Music* have been recast, sometimes beyond recognition.
- The first essay is new, as are the headnotes and the final poem.
- Poems of mine I refer to can be found in *Heart Residence* (Anansi, 2017).

Toronto, 2025

Part I

Wrestling with Cadence

I WAS SITTING WITH FRIENDS IN A SMALL TORONTO RESTAURANT, just off Yorkville Avenue. This was back in the 1970s. And something happened that would become a touchstone in my writing.

As the four of us nattered away, I realized that my body had started to vibrate. Faintly but unmistakably — a slow, repeated throb. What was going on?

I asked the waiter. And he told us there was a studio in the basement where a rock band practised; in fact, they were going at it as we spoke. The studio was soundproofed, so nothing was audible. But the pulsation of the electric bass made the beams and girders vibrate. And the pulse travelled up through the frame of the two-storey building, activating the floor of the restaurant ... the benches where we sat ... and finally, us.

We had become a kinesthetic extension of the music, or at least of the bass line. Our bodies were collateral instruments.

◆

I thought of the Yorkville vibration recently, when the editor at Stonehewer Books made an urgent request. Could I please tell readers what *Wrestling with Cadence* is about? The essays keep returning to something I call "cadence." But despite all my descriptions, the editor still couldn't fathom what cadence *is*. He'd never had the kind of experience I speak of, and the standard definitions of cadence didn't seem to apply. So could I take pity on the reader? Spell out exactly what cadence consists of?

It was true: I had expanded the normal meaning of the word. So I promised to try. And maybe the story of the Yorkville vibration could start things off — as a down-to-earth parallel, which readers would get right away.

◆

I worked on my first poetry collection, *Kingdom of Absence,* for seven years. And it was a dud. The poems were more or less sonnets, though they often broke the rules; I was both following the conventions of the form, and pushing against them. But there was no real point to the exercise, and meanwhile the voice felt cramped and abstract. Here's a sample quatrain:

> We explicate the trees but they go sorrowing
> mutely beyond us, botched in our dimension.
> Rilke, master of ripeness, and the things'
> celebrant, rapt, be near to us in limbo. ...

The book finally limped into print in 1967. And with that, I started paying closer attention to something I'd been dimly aware of for some time — a tumble of rhythms and hunches. Or to speak more accurately — a tumble of wordless energies, erupting and criss-crossing in a space I couldn't identify, but which was unmistakably there. I'd felt it thrumming for years, but I'd been too trapped in this constricted poetic voice to do anything about it.

Mind you, I had made a few attempts. I have a fragmentary memory from back then, and it still gives me a pang. There was a shock of recognition I experienced whenever I read Gerard Manley

Hopkins, and likewise with the German poet Friedrich Hölderlin. Their torrential rhythms felt like home. But how did they *do* it? I decided (in this snippet of memory) to find out for myself; maybe I could follow their lead.

So I'm reading a poem I love (by Hopkins? by Hölderlin?) — hoping that its headlong rhythmic power will rub off on me. I mark the strong and weak stresses, syllable by syllable, from beginning to end. And then I compose a poem of my own — with the spoken stresses of my text (the strong and weak inflections of conversational English) arranged to match each strong or weak stress in the original. I'm juiced ... this is down-in-the-trenches research ... it feels like I'm cracking the code ...

I knew so little then. True, I did reproduce the rhythmic specs of a marvellous poem. But I could tell that my version was dead on arrival. It just sat there. And so, while my contemporaries were making notable debuts all around me, I went back to my bastardized sonnets. Haunted by rhythms I could sense, but couldn't get anywhere close to in words.

◆

But in the spring of 1967, with *Kingdom of Absence* finally off my back, things changed. I had resigned from teaching at the University of Toronto; I was embarking on what proved to be a two-year stint at the experimental Rochdale College, and a five-year stint at a new literary press, Anansi.

And I had returned to my rhythmic groping — hoping (once again) that the movement of words on the page could re-enact the lunges and skitters and swoops I kept sensing. But I still didn't have the foggiest idea what such poetry would look like; I'd given up trying to replicate Hopkins and Hölderlin, and I was on my own. So all through that summer I sat up, night after night — letting the pen go wherever it wanted, say whatever it had to. In a kind of blind automatic writing. And somehow, during those months, the breakthrough occurred; the rhythmic tumult I'd been hankering for came pouring through. The result was *Civil Elegies*, published in 1968, where a poem could move like this:

> I come to the square each time there is nothing and once, made calm again
> by the spare vertical glory of right proportions,
> watching the wind cut loose as it riffled the clouds on the skyline, framing the
>   towers at noon,
> catching the newsboys' raucous cry of race in the streets and the war and
>   Confederation going,
> smelling the air, the interminable stink of production and transport and
> caught once more in the square's great hush with the shoppers, hippies, brokers,
>   children, old men dozing alone by the pool and waiting ...

A few years later, at a writers' conference in Montreal, I tried to describe the field of energies that had catalyzed these new poems. But as I soon realized, there was no way to even refer to it. We don't have a word in English for "an array of blurts & squirts of non-verbal energy that take you over but they can't be seen or heard by anyone else." But I had to call the fool thing *something*. So I hijacked the closest term I could think of — "cadence." There was nothing sacrosanct about the word, though; I could have called it Fred.

◆

But this won't satisfy my editor, because I still haven't addressed the obvious questions. Is the thing I call cadence real? And if it is, where does it exist? In my head? Out in the world? In some woo-woo mystical dimension? What on earth *is* it?

The truth is, I can't answer those questions. So I invite you to pause with me, and consider what other people have experienced along the same lines. Such accounts aren't widespread; if we consider the population at large, relatively few people report anything of this kind. But when they do, there are certain features that recur.

Consider the great Russian poet, Osip Mandelstam. In a memoir, *Hope Against Hope*, his widow Nadezhda describes how Mandelstam worked. The first stirrings of a poem always came as a wordless "hum":

> As many poets have said — Akhmatova (in "Poem Without a Hero") and M. among them — a poem begins with a musical phrase ringing insistently in the ears; at first inchoate, it later takes on a precise form, though still without words. I sometimes saw M. trying to get rid of this kind of "hum," to brush it off and escape from it. He would toss his head as though it could be shaken out like a drop of water that gets into your ear while bathing.
>
> The "hum" sometimes came to M. in his sleep, but he could never remember it on waking. ... The whole process of composition is one of straining to catch and record something compounded of harmony and sense as it is relayed from an unknown source and gradually forms itself into words. ...
>
> Whenever M.'s "inner voice" ceased, he was always very eager to read the new poem to someone. I wasn't enough for this: I witnessed his throes at such close quarters that M. always thought I must also be able to hear the "hum."

That's a graphic example of what we commonly call *intuition*. And Nadezhda's account can serve as a kind of informal template; things she points to appear in other examples too. They include the following:

- The intuitive experience is self-certifying. Mandelstam can no more doubt the reality of the hum than question the reality of a table or chair in his room. In this respect, the hum is like the Yorkville vibration; it validates itself by its sheer presence.

- But the hum arises from "an unknown source." Unlike the throbbing in the restaurant, it can't be traced to a physical cause; nor can anyone else hear it. Its provenance is a blank.
- Mandelstam isn't awestruck by these visitations; he seems more inclined to greet them with exasperation. And then, quite matter-of-factly, he gets to work on the poem.
- In its initial manifestation, the hum is formless, undifferentiated, a kind of teeming blur. In Nadezhda's term, it's "inchoate."
- The blur takes the form of a "musical phrase." It has no verbal content — or not at first. That will emerge only later, as the hum "gradually forms itself into words."
- To jump ahead slightly: despite what Nadezhda says, the intuitive ruckus can be mediated by various sense organs. But these aren't the faculties we use in regular perception. For Mandelstam, it's what we call the inner ear. For others, it's the eye of the mind, the third eye. For still others it may be the sense of touch, or even the whole body — though still not in its everyday, physical mode.

And a technical point. We need a general, catch-all term for this something-or-other that intrudes. We can't refer to it as "the hum," or "cadence"; those are names for specific cases. So, *faute de mieux*, I'll dub the phenomenon the "intuitive field."

◆

Now consider the English poet and playwright John Dryden. His poetry could hardly be more unlike Mandelstam's. But look at the Dedication to his 1664 play, *The Rival Ladies*. He's addressing the dedicatee, the Earl of Orrery:

> This worthless present was designed [for] you long before it was a play; when it was only a confused mass of thoughts, tumbling over one another in the dark; when the fancy was yet in its first work, moving the sleeping images of things towards the light.

For Dryden, the intuitive field begins as the familiar blurry matrix. And he describes the "confused mass" as made up of "thoughts" — which might imply at least a semi-verbal tinge. But his dominant sense is clearly the eye, and the visual aspect is much stronger than anything to do with language. The elements "tumble over one another in the dark," and he has to "move the sleeping images of things towards the light." He registers the whole thing visually, not aurally or linguistically.

The most intriguing moment comes a bit later. Dryden tells the Earl:

> I confess, in that first tumult of my thoughts, there appeared a disorderly kind of beauty in some of them, which gave me hope, something worthy my lord of Orrery might be drawn from them. But ... when I had moulded it into that shape it now bears, I looked with such disgust upon it, that the censures of our severest critics are charitable [compared] to what I thought (and still think) of it myself.

This is not the standard, aw-shucks-it-was-nothing demurral. It has the bite of genuine revulsion. The original vision had a "disorderly kind of beauty," which far surpasses whatever Dryden has managed to bring across.

◆

It's not just writers who work intuitively, nor even artists in general. Think of Richard Feynman, the American physicist who's often described as the most creative theorist since Einstein. Feynman relied on intuition, and his receiving apparatus was complex. As his biographer James Gleick remarks, his "intuition was not just visual but also auditory and kinesthetic."

Let's start with the kinesthetic. For Feynman, thinking about some intractable problem in physics involved finding a deeper approach to the problem than was currently available. This called for resources beyond the purely rational. And his whole body became the setting in which intuition occurred:

> Those who watched Feynman in moments of intense concentration came away with a strong, even disturbing sense of the physicality of the process, as though his brain did not stop with the gray matter but extended through every muscle in his body. A Cornell dormitory neighbor opened Feynman's door to find him rolling about on the floor beside his bed as he worked on a problem.

Or the intuitive nudges might arrive in auditory form:

> His Los Alamos colleagues were sometimes amused to hear him, when thinking out loud, howl a sort of whooping glissando when he meant, *this rises exponentially*; a different sound signified *arithmetically*.

But Feynman's deepest intuitive mode was visual. When he was exploring a complex problem, he would start by calling up a visual field in his mind's eye. Here's how he described the process that followed: "What I am really trying to do is bring birth to clarity, which is really a half-assedly thought-out pictorial semi-vision thing. ... It's all visual. It's hard to explain."

This less-than-helpful explication is worth examining more closely. Feynman might be trying to solve a knotty problem in quantum mechanics. But what occupied his attention was this intuitive visual field, whose elements somehow embodied what he was wrestling with. It included flickering colours, adjustable shapes, and Rube Goldberg–like collapsible combinations that he would fiddle and twiddle with in his mind's eye, trying to make the picture feel right.

The process was only partly comprehensible to his colleagues, and it's completely incomprehensible to the rest of us. But one thing stands out, even to a layperson. We saw how Mandelstam's intuitive hunches were pre-verbal at first. The musical hum formed itself only gradually into words, and by then much of the heavy lifting had been accomplished. In similar fashion, Feynman's intuitive explorations were pre-mathematical at first. Only later would they resolve into the symbols and procedures of higher mathematics. In one interview, he spoke of the process as "an inspired method of picturing, I guess. Ordinarily I try to get the pictures clearer, but in the end the mathematics can take over and be more efficient in communicating the idea of the picture." Some of the seminal advances in modern physics were made during these painstaking joyrides in the intuitive field.

◆

These samples demonstrate the wide variety of intuitive experience. And if we go back to the "informal template" we coaxed out of Mandelstam's practice, we can now add to it. Albeit in a provisional spirit; this is hardly an exhaustive survey.

- The intuitive field can appear in at least three modes: visual, auditory, and kinesthetic.
- The mode in which it first appears may not be the one the person actually works in. In which case, there will be a transition to their home medium — later in the process, and apparently with no special effort.

We could call this unusual feature a "crossover." It occurs unmistakably with Mandelstam (going from a musical phrase to words), and with Feynman (going from visual imagery to mathematics). It's unclear whether such a crossover takes place with Dryden.

◆

We've taken the long way round, but I can finally respond to my editor's request. Meaning, I can situate cadence within a coherent larger picture.

Cadence is one manifestation of the "intuitive field," which barges in on some people who do creative work, and propels them in unexpected directions. I still can't say where it comes from, and I still don't know what it is. But my encounters with cadence echo what other people have experienced in *their* disciplines. The details differ, but the fundamental experience is consistent — as our template showed.

So the key fact about cadence is that the class or category it belongs to is "the intuitive field." That tells us what kind of a thing it is. And if the whole phenomenon remains mysterious after that, the mystery has at least taken on a recognizable shape and hue. Which may be the fullest explanation my editor can hope for.

◆

But there are other questions to ask, apart from "What *is* it?" Practical questions.

When cadence barrelled into my poetry, back in the summer of 1967, it arrived as a major breakthrough — something I had never experienced till then. And it was inscrutable. I've been wrestling with cadence ever since, however, and that's something I *can* speak about. So: are there questions about the day-to-day wrestle? ... Anyone?

Here's something I was wondering about, Mr. Lee. You gave

examples where people hear *the "intuitive field." Or sometimes they* see *it. But how does it appear to you?*

Well, I don't perceive cadence visually, and the auditory sense is secondary. For me, it's the kinesthetic faculty that takes the lead.

When all this started, the energy field that took hold *was* kinesthetic. That was the given, and I was at home with it. It was like the Yorkville vibration, without the rock band. But at the same time, I knew doodly-squat *about* kinesthesia. It operates in hidden places, and it's only recently that we've had the technology to explore it up close. And I've discovered *[Uh-oh! He's going off on a tangent]* that we have these tiny sensors, called "proprioceptors," in our muscles and joints. They report to the central nervous system about things inside the body — things like muscular stress, balance, motion, and so forth. And we process similar information as we move around in space — getting nerve-end reports from our skin, plus input from our eyes and ears. The kinesthetic network is amazing; it serves as a full-tilt communication system within the body.

But that's the *physical* kinesthetic sense. When it comes to intuitive perception, it's a faculty of a different kind. We don't have a catchy moniker for "the intuitive kinesthetic sense." But it's just as real as the mind's eye, or the inner ear.

All that said *[Whew! This may be the end of the tangent],* my experience of cadence isn't centred on the body alone. It's attuned to the wider space my body's embedded in. It comes through mainly to the right of my body — I have no idea why. And it presents itself, not just as a jostle of movements going every whichway, but as an arena of shifting *textures* too — curlicue wisps, tight bunchings, stentorian chunks. All of them fluctuating.

So it's this larger dance of energies that compels me — that I hanker to recreate in the movement and texture of words on the page. In the poem's *voice.*

Mr. Lee, you spoke of a "major breakthrough." Does this mean you get a breakthrough every time you work on a poem?

Hang on a minute. Like I said: with a poem, it's a matter of *voice*. Kinesthetic voice, if that makes any sense. That's what I work on, after the muscular *hoo-ha* comes through. It's how the intuitive field leaves its imprint on a poem. ... Come to think of it, that's another example of the crossover. You start off tracking intuitive bodily energies, which are pre-verbal; you end up with multi-textured words on the page. For whatever reason, the intuitive field may not come through in your normal working medium, when it first kicks in.

And no — these seismic breakthroughs aren't daily events. A *breakthrough* means that some entirely new voice has taken hold. It's unlike anything I've written before; it's delivered in already-achieved form, or something close to it; and it's as unexpected to me as to anybody else. In sixty-plus years of scribbling, I've had exactly three such major breakthroughs.

What were they? When did they happen?

The first was with *Civil Elegies* — in 1967, in Toronto. Then *Riffs* — in 1981, in Edinburgh. And then with *Un* — in 2000, in Barcelona. The rest of my writing life (after the dismal seven years at the start) has been spent catching up with those new voices. Exploring the possibilities, till there was nothing left to discover. And then I spun my wheels, hoping for another breakthrough — which was out of my control, so good luck.

But what does *happen when you're working on a poem? Every day, I mean. Do you still rely on your theory of cadence?*

No no *no*! Haven't you been — ? ... Oh, man ...

Let's pause for a second. I don't rely on my theory of cadence, because I don't *have* a theory of cadence. All I have is the bare-naked *experience* of cadence — it's what I live by as a poet. If I based my stuff on some theory about cadence, it would mean I'd never actually done time with the damn thing, getting goosed into words.

Okay, back to your question. What happens day by day? I can tune in to cadence almost any time, just by sitting still. But after a major breakthrough, and once I get attuned to it, the clues I pick up are more local. More piecemeal. If I get a few words right, that's a good day's work; if a run of six lines clicks into phase with itself, that's a bonanza. So after one of these breakthroughs, I have to be satisfied with small, incremental steps. ... Needless to say, this is just one man's experience. And like most writers, I've cobbled things together by trial and error. Probably no two people who work intuitively have the same day-to-day practice.

What about the content*? Does cadence tell you what a poem should be about?*

Well, no and yes. I often start with a brilliant idea for what to write about. But then I get a sense for the rhythmic lingo of the piece, or maybe a phrase pops up and it feels right. And as that begins to knit together, it may have nothing to do with whatever subject I had in mind at the outset. And the more elaborate the scaffolding is — of my preconceptions about the content, I mean — the more energy I have to spend, prying the poem free from the wretched scaffolding.

Sometimes I wish I knew the ground rules for a given poem ahead of time, instead of just groping around in the dark. But the truth is, I love it this way. Panic is a poet's best friend.

But don't you get some kind of positive feeling, when you're on the right track?

With the full-scale breakthroughs, my first reaction was more like an anxiety attack. What *is* this stuff? It sure doesn't look like poetry. ... But then you start to adjust.

And after that, there are smaller epiphanies that come along — for minor advances. They arrive with a feeling of certainty: "Yes! This is *it!*" But the odd thing is, the same feeling of certainty accompanies an epiphany when it's ill-judged, or incomplete, or flat-out wrong. So there has to be a certain testing of the Ah-*ha!* moments. Some epiphanies stand up to scrutiny; others fizzle out.

Let me change the subject. Does your ordinary body feel the muscle sensations that you intuit? Like Mandelstam's did, when he heard the hum?

Only faintly. ... No, that's not right. I experience the swooping and clenching first-hand. But it's not in my physical body — I don't know where it is. There's also a certain amount of bobbing around and body English that come with it. But that's like an echo, or a companionable accompaniment.

I'm changing the subject here too. I was wondering — can this happen to anybody? This, whatever-you-call-it?

Well, the experience isn't all that frequent, as far as I can tell. And it can't be conjured up by willpower. But it comes to men and women of genius, and it comes to lesser mortals too. So it doesn't seem to depend on having off-the-charts talent.

But it does seem arbitrary. I don't understand why some good writers experience a version of the intuitive field, and other good writers don't appear to. There are different kinds of excellence, I guess.

One last question. What's the difference between artistic inspiration, which is a commonly understood concept, and the kind of intuition you're talking about?

Whoa! That's a ... *[Drums fingers.]*

Okay, first thought: there *is* no difference. "Inspiration" and "the intuitive field" are different names for the same thing; they just come at it from different angles.

But I like the question. I like the idea that there's more than one way that artists or scientists can get propelled into a new take on things. So let's try a thought experiment. Suppose there's a Type A, and a Type B. What is the key element that distinguishes A from B?

Both can produce superb work; both are intuitive/inspired to beat the band. So why do they belong in different categories?

Let's sketch the two types.

When inspiration strikes Type A, it's incandescent — and it's a done deal from the start. It comes to them in a flash. And it arrives in the same format or medium they'll use in the finished work — be it words, or musical notes, or images. So what takes hold of them is the complete work, delivered in their natural medium.

Mozart was a classic Type A. He'd go out for a walk after dinner, and come home with a new symphony in his head — with every note for every instrument in place. That's what came to him, and it was in musical form from the start. So he'd simply transcribe the entire work, and go to bed.

Now look at Type B. When inspiration strikes, it's incandescent too. But there's a difference. The kindling takes place in a different medium from the one B normally works in. It begins as a musical hum for Mandelstam; as a picture for Feynman; and (if I can include myself among the examples) as kinesthetic noodling for me. So the inspiration is completed only when the crossover takes place; it's not direct. And it may take longer for it all to unfold — I don't know enough about the two processes to make a comparison.

Nobody gets to choose which type they are. And neither one is better than the other. But they're not the same thing. And if we're looking to get a handle on the intuitive field, this might be a useful distinction.

When it comes to the essays in *Wrestling with Cadence,* bear in mind that they were all written by a dyed-in-the-wool Type B. I can't hold forth about Mozartian inspiration, since I don't experience it.

But you play the hand you're dealt. And I've been lucky.

2025

Cadence, Country, Silence:
Writing in Colonial Space

This began as a ten-minute talk at a writers' conference in Montreal, back in 1972. The theme was "L'écriture et l'errance" — "Writing and Wandering." And the wording puzzled me; what were we supposed to talk about?

The first evening was the customary social mixer, and I kept asking people about the theme. I discovered that écriture *and* errance *were buzzwords from the latest new thing in Paris — postmodernism, about which I knew zilch at the time. Beyond that clue, I met with nothing but amiable shrugs; it was evidently far too complicated to explain in a few words.*

But I still had to say something *in my talk the next day. Back in my room, I took hurried stock of my adventures and misadventures in writing — thinking some of it through for the first time. That would have to do for* errance. *And I conscripted the term "cadence," to designate a pre-verbal energy that had waylaid me in 1967, and led to* Civil Elegies. *Maybe that could qualify as* écriture.

I no longer recall what I said in my ten-minute ramble. But it furnished a roadmap for "Cadence, Country, Silence," which I pulled together for the published proceedings of the conference. To my surprise, it would become — in successive versions — the most widely circulated of all my essays.

1. Cadence

MOST OF MY TIME AS A POET IS SPENT LISTENING INTO A luminous tumble, a sort of taut cascade. I call it *cadence.* If I withdraw from immediate contact with things around me, I can sense it churning, flickering, thrumming. What I hear is initially without words; but when a poem starts to come, the words have to accord with that magisterial flux, or I can't make the poem at all.

I speak of "hearing" cadence, but the sensation isn't auditory. It's more like sensing a constantly changing tremor with your body — a play of movement and stress, torsion and flex. More and more I sense this energy as presence, both outside and inside myself. I take my vocation to consist of listening into it with enough life concentration that it can become words.

◆

I first became conscious of cadence in my twenties. The experience was elusive but unmistakable; I was embedded, as plainly as I was in the earth's atmosphere, in a kinesthetic space which was alive and volatile. If I sat quietly, I became aware of this pre-verbal field of force. It had no specific content, or none to begin with. It was its own content, a rich symphony of clenching and swoops. Sometimes I went for weeks without attending to it, but I believe it continued its judder and carom and chug without me.

And while this didn't jibe with anything I knew about writing, it was too immediate to deny. A poem was meant to enact what cadence had been doing all along — not by describing it, but by reliving its muscular trajectories in words. And compared to that challenge, the chance to turn a good phrase, compose deft verses, the chance to "be a poet," left me cold. It seemed like the cheapest evasion. For this jazzy, majestic, delicately cascading process I heard surging and pausing and thudding was without the witness I might be, if it chose to animate my words.

I don't say that with any false humility, for I'm convinced it does choose to. But it impresses me with the dumbness of most of what a writer is tempted to do, and it leaves me impatient that I can't organize my life so as to listen with greater concentration.

◆

The first catalyst was Friedrich Hölderlin. I discovered his poetry in my early twenties, in a course called something like "Goethe and His Contemporaries," and it changed my sense of how words can move on the page. And shortly after, I started getting intimations of a music — not his — which I could feel bucking and swivelling just outside my conscious perception. But the nudgings didn't lead to anything concrete; my own apprentice poetry was stuck in a creakily traditional prosody, and I couldn't free it up.

In fact, I spent seven years composing a sequence of sonnet variations, *Kingdom of Absence.* Listen to one of these pieces:

> When I review my troop of scruffy selves
> and count personae, when I hear the tramp
> of brawling cells in whichway phalanx wheeling,
> spun by every creak of the swivelling wind,
>
> and when I see the sleek and shifty mind
> doing his pander, and the awkward-squad volitions
> fresh from screwing with his fair daughters,
> I flinch that I must answer their salute. ...

The sonnet goes on, but I'll stop there. So much is wrong — the stagey extended metaphor; the overly-conscious mix of high and low diction; the speaker's knee-jerk despair — that a reader might not pick up on what appalls me most. Which is, its way of hearing rhythm. This is an ear that no longer hears metrically — or not with subtlety and bite, as in the great tradition from Chaucer to Yeats. But neither has it discovered an alternate way of scoring the procession of syllables. So it just thumps along, trapped in the latter-day decadence of the iambic pentameter line.

And the larger rhythmic moves are equally out of sync with themselves. Whatever exploratory energy may be operating here, it almost certainly doesn't want to proceed within the tight sonnet structure. But it has taken refuge there, and the structure becomes a straitjacket — no matter how many cosmetic liberties the poet takes.

It wasn't until the sequence was finally published that things would change.

◆

I still remember the summer of 1967. *Kingdom of Absence* had just appeared. And almost at once, the rhythms I'd sensed for so long erupted into words.

The new voice could sound like this:

> It would be better maybe if we could stop loving the children
> and their delicate brawls, pelting across the square in tandem, deking
> from cover to cover in raucous celebration and they are never
> winded, bemusing us with the rites of our own
> gone childhood; if only they stopped
> mattering, the children, it might be possible, now
> while the square lies stunned by noon. ...

I found myself scrambling night after night to keep up with these hurtling lines. They were no longer clumping through pre-set metrical patterns; they moved with an almost-off-balance gait which seemed to emerge directly from the cascade of energy. I remember sitting up each night in a kind of dictation high — cowed but exhilarated by the music that had taken me over. It kept coming, and the first version of *Civil Elegies* appeared in 1968.

But then something bizarre happened: I dried. For the next three years, I couldn't write a thing that rang true; twenty words on a page would set me wincing at their palpable falsity. I still went into my study and doodled, but I wound up scrapping everything I wrote. And I had no notion where the music had gone. The block was as unexpected as the breakthrough had been.

I have a better sense of it now. There was a longstanding check on my pen, which returned shortly after cadence declared itself. There were old dues still to be paid.

2. Country

To get at this complex situation, I need to explore how cadence can be blocked at deeper levels than the personal. If we live in a common space which is radically in question for us, that makes our barest speaking problematic to itself. For voice does issue in part from civil space. And alienation in that space will enter and undercut our writing, make it recoil upon itself, become a problem to itself.

What does that sentence mean? Writing "becomes a problem to itself" when there's a vicious circle: when to write calls for something that makes writing impossible. Contradictions in our public belonging are one thing that has that effect. And for an English Canadian, exploring civil obstructions to writing means exploring the nature of colonial space. For the prime fact about my country today is that it has become an American client state. But we speak the same tongue as our new masters, and the way this undercuts our writing isn't easy to discern.

Let me return to my early experience. I began writing seriously about 1960, when I was twenty-one. My sense at the time was that I had access to a great many words: those of the British tradition, the American, and — insofar as anyone took it seriously — the Canadian. (When I speak of "words," I mean all the resources of the verbal imagination — from nouns and verbs to structures of plot and versions of the hero). Yet at the same time those words seemed to lie in a random heap, which glittered with promise so long as I considered it in the mass, but within which each individual word went stiff, inert, was somehow clogged with sludge, the moment I tried to move it into a poem. I could stir words, prod them, wedge them into place. But there was no way I could speak them freely as my own.

Writers everywhere don't begin with an external, resistant language; something more was involved than just getting the hang of the medium during apprenticeship. In any case, after I'd published the first book and finished the second, I stopped being able to use words on paper at all. Everywhere around me — in England, the States, even Canada — writers opened their mouths and words spilled out like crazy. But I just choked. And looking back at my first book, I felt as if I'd been fishing pretty beads out of a vat of crankcase oil, and stringing them together. The words weren't limber, or alive, or even mine.

◆

Though I didn't realize it at the time, I was suffering the recoil from something Canadians had learned profoundly after World War II — certainly in southern Ontario, the region where I grew up. To want our lives to become articulate in books, in movies, in songs — that was ridiculous, uppity. Canadians were by definition people who looked over the fence at America, unself-consciously learning from its comics, pop music, and television how to go about being alive. The disdainful amusement I and thousands like me felt for Canadian achievement in any field, especially those of the imagination, was a direct reflection of this sense of inferiority. And while we sneered at American mass culture, we could distance ourselves from it only by soaking up the countervailing American culture: Mailer and Fiedler and Baldwin, the hip and the Beats. This was between (say) 1955 and 1965.

And like sellouts everywhere, we were prepared to capitulate, not for a cut of the action, but simply on condition that we not be humiliated by being lumped with the rest of the natives. We were desperate to make that clear: we weren't like the rest. And we fell all over ourselves, putting down the Canadians. The fact that we would never meet the Americans we admired didn't cramp our style. We felt inferior anyway, and we compensated like mad. We kept up with *The Paris Review* and *Partisan*; we shook our heads over how Senator McCarthy had perverted our finest traditions; in some cases we went down to Washington to confront the government about the Vietnam War. It boggles the mind, but that was what we did — it's how we *felt*. We weren't pretending, we were desperate. And the idea that these things only confirmed our colonialism would have made us laugh our continentalized heads off. We weren't all that clear on colonialism to begin with, but if anybody had it, it was our countrymen, the Canadians, who in some unspecified way were still in thrall to England. But *we* weren't colonials; hell, we could have held up our heads in New York. Though it was a relief that no one asked us to.

◆

My awakening from this supine condition was private, and extremely disorienting. It was touched off by the American critique of America during the Vietnam War. But it ended up going much further. From that muddled process I remember a couple of months in 1965, after a teach-in at the University of Toronto. It lasted a weekend, and as I followed the long, dull speeches in Varsity Arena, two things dawned on me. The first was that the American government had been lying about the war — on a colossal scale. And the second was that the Canadian media, from which I'd learned most of what I knew about Vietnam, were spreading its lies.

I present these discoveries in all the crashing naïveté with which they struck me then. And while the first revelation shocked me more at the time — the lies about America's imperial disaster — it was the second revelation that gnawed at me during the ensuing months. I couldn't get my mind around it. I didn't believe that Canadian newspapers and television had been bought off directly by Washington — given cash to promote the war. But if it was not a case of paid corruption, the only reason for cooperating in such blatant deception — consciously or not — was that they were colonial media, serving the interests of the imperial rulers.

Mind you, that language made me twitch. It conjured up images of five-hour harangues in Havana and Peking; I'd read about *that* in our papers too. But no matter; it was the only language that made sense of what was happening.

Even worse, I had to recognize that the imperial influence was not confined to the media. It also included my head. More and more of the ideas I had, my assumptions, even the instinctive path of my feelings, seemed to have come north from the States unexamined. That had once been what I strove for. But now the whole thing had turned around, and I was jarred loose. After ten years of continentalizing my ass, what had I accomplished?

I was a colonial.

It was during this murky, drawn-out process that I began to find literary words impossible. I didn't know why. But writing had become a full-fledged problem to itself. It had grown into a search for authenticity, but all it could be was a symptom of inauthenticity. I could feel that with every nerve end in my body. And so for three years, I shut up.

◆

It was when I read a series of essays by the philosopher George Grant that I began to comprehend our condition. His analysis of "Canadian Fate and Imperialism," which I read in 1967 in *Canadian Dimension*, was the first that made any contact with my tenuous sense of living here — the first in which I recognized the words of our civil estate. My whole system had been coiling in on itself for want of them. As subsequent pieces appeared (they were collected in 1969 as *Technology and Empire*, the book of Grant's from which I learned most deeply), I realized that somehow it had happened. A man who knew this paralyzing condition first-hand was nonetheless using words authentically, from the centre of everything that had tied my tongue.

One central perception was that, in refusing the American dream, our Loyalist forebears — the British Americans who came north after 1776 — were groping to preserve a classical European tradition, which taught that reverence is more fully human than conquest or mastery. That we are subject to sterner necessities than liberty and the pursuit of happiness — that we must respond, as best we can, to the demands of the good. (Grant didn't claim that all Hellenic and Christian societies had lived up to those ideals, only that they understood themselves to be acting well or badly in their light.) I knew that the Loyalists were not a homogeneous group, and that many had come north for the main chance. Yet convictions like these demonstrably underlay many of their attitudes to Europe, to law, the land, Indigenous peoples. Their refusal of America issued, in part, from a disagreement about what it meant to be human.

What the Loyalists were refusing was the doctrine of radical freedom, which in an argument of inspired simplicity Grant sees as the point of generation of technological civilization. That doctrine led to a view of everything but our naked wills — the new continent, native peoples, other nations, outer space, even our own bodies — as raw material, to be manipulated according to our desires and the dictates of our technology. But not only did this view of an unlimited freedom seem arrogant, even suicidal; it was just plain wrong. For we are *not* radically free, in point of fact. And to act as if we are is to behave with lethal naïveté.

Mind you, this overstates what Grant finds in the Loyalists. In fact, he declares that the typical Loyalist was "straight Locke with a dash of Anglicanism"; the British tradition he held to had already broken with the classical understanding of the good. Loyalism was a gesture in the right direction, perhaps, but it never succeeded in being radically un-American. It didn't have the resources to re-constitute modernity.

◆

This undercutting of a past he would have liked to make exemplary is a characteristic moment in Grant's thought, and it reveals the central strength and contradiction of his work. He withdraws from the contemporary world, and judges it with passionate lucidity, by standing on a fixed point — the primacy of the good — which he then reveals to be no longer there. Or at the least, to be no longer accessible to the modern mind. This way of proceeding makes his thought difficult to live with, a fact which his own best work explores rigorously.

I found this account of being alive far less indulgent than the liberal version that achieved its zenith in America — far closer to the way things actually are. Now there were terms in which to recognize that, as we began to criticize our new masters during the 1960s, we were not just hoping to be nicer Americans, to dream their dream more humanely. Our dissent went as deep as it did because, obscurely, we did not want to be American at all. Their dream was wrong.

Before Grant, a person who'd grown up in as deeply colonized a decade as the 1950s had no access to such a conscious refusal of America. Our tiresome beginnings had always been a source of embarrassment: no revolution, no Wild West frontier, no six-gun heroes. As this mindset was stood on its head, Grant gave us access to our origins. And going further, he acknowledged the primacy of Indigenous peoples and their ways of being — a striking recognition at the time. Yet he also considered their chthonic wisdom to be beyond the ken of those who were not Indigenous.

But Grant is scarcely an apostle of public joy. By now, he says, we have replaced our forebears' tentative, dissenting space with a wholehearted American one. The sellout of Canada which has been consummated over the last few decades does not involve just natural resources or corporate takeovers, nor who will put the marionettes in Ottawa through their paces. It replaces one way of being human with another.

For the political and military rule of the United States, and the economic rule of its corporations, are merely the surface expression of modernity in the West. That modernity is also inward. It shapes the expression of our bodies' impulses, the way we build cities, what we do with our spare time. Always we are totally free agents, faced with a world which is raw material, a permanent incitement to technique. There is no court of appeal outside that circuit. And even though we can observe this worldview destroying the planet, that doesn't give us access to a different worldview.

Hence to dissent from liberal modernity is to fall silent, for we have no terms in which to speak that do not replicate the very assumptions we're trying to speak against. We may sense "intimations of deprival" to which modernity is not open, but we can sense them only inarticulately. Grant explores this impasse with a clarity which induces vertigo.

I recognize all the bleakness for which he is often criticized. But only with my head. For months after I read Grant's essays, I felt a surge of release and exhilaration. To find one's tongue-tied sense of civil loss and bafflement given words at last, to hear one's inarticulate hunches out loud, because most immediate in the bloodstream — and not prettied up, and in prose like a fastidious groundswell — was to stand erect at last in one's own place.

I don't expect to spend my lifetime agreeing with George Grant. But in my experience, the sombre Canadian has enabled us to say for the first time where we are, who we are — to become articulate. That gift of speech is a staggering achievement. And in trying to comprehend the deeper ways in which writing is a problem to itself in Canada, I start with Grant.

◆

Why did I dry? We're getting closer to the centre of the tangle.

The words I knew said Britain, and they said the States. But they did not say my home. They were always and only about other people's lives. All the rich structures of language were available, but the currents that animated them were not native to the people who use the language here. Let alone to those who were here before us.

But the civil self seeks nourishment as much as the biological. And if everything it has ready access to is alien, it may protect itself in a visceral spasm of refusal. To take an immediate example: the words I used above — "language," "home," "here" — have no Canadian charge. They convey only the meanings in whose face we have been unable to find ourselves since the beginning. This is not to call for arbitrary new Canadian definitions, of course. It's simply to point out that the texture, weight, and connotation of almost every word we use comes from abroad. For a person who wants to recreate our being human here in words — and where else do we live? — that creates a radical impasse. Writing has become a problem to itself at the most basic level.

Why did I dry?

The language was drenched with our nonbelonging. And words — bizarre as it sounds, even to myself — words had become the enemy. To use them was to collaborate further in one's extinction as a rooted human being. And so, by a drastic and involuntary stratagem of self-preserval, words went dead.

◆

The first necessity for a colonial writer — so runs the conventional wisdom — is to write about what they know. The imagination must come home. But that necessity is not enough. For if you are Canadian, home is the place that is not home to you — it is even less your home than the imperial centre you dream about. Or to say what I really know: the *words* of home are silent. And to raise a stirring classical ode to the harvests of Saskatchewan, or to set a noir murder mystery in Newfoundland, is no answer at all. Try to speak the words of your home and you will discover, if you are a colonial, that you do not know them. You are left chafing at the inarticulacy of a native space that may not even exist. So you shut up.

◆

But perhaps — and here was the breakthrough — perhaps our job was not to fake a space of our own and write it up, but rather to speak the words of our spacelessness. Perhaps that *was* home. This dawned on me gradually. Instead of pushing against the grain of our wordless condition, perhaps we should come to writing *with* that grain.

To do so was a homecoming — and a thoroughly iffy homecoming it was. In the 1960s, it meant giving up the notion of writing in the same continuum as Lowell, Ginsberg, Olson, Plath, Hughes. Yet it was not a matter of taking an easier road; finding your own voice would be chancier than echoing theirs. Rather, it meant assuming that what is for real can be claimed by a Canadian in the language of their own time and place. If they can learn to speak that language. And so you began striving to hear what happened in words — in "love," "inhabit," "fail," "earth," "home" — as you let them surface in your mute and native land. This was an eerie, visceral process; there were no signposts, only the will to let words be how they are for us.

But I'm distorting the experience again by writing it down. There was nothing conscious about this, initially at least; it was simply a direction my inner ear took. I know I resisted.

◆

The first mark of words, as you began to re-hear them in this empty civil space, was the blur of unachieved meaning. That much I knew already. But the oppressiveness started to change, for I could sense something more.

Where I lived, a whole swarm of inarticulate meanings lunged, clawed, drifted, eddied, sprawled in half-grasped disarray beneath the tidy meaning which the simplest word brought with it from England and the States. *City*: once you accepted the featureless character of that word — responding to it as a Canadian noun, with its absence of native connotation — you were dimly savaged by the live, inchoate meanings trying to surface through it. The whole tangle and Sisyphean problematic of settlers' existence here, from the time of the *coureurs de bois* to the present day, came struggling to be included in "city." Cooped up beneath the familiar surface of the word as we use it (city as London, Paris, New York) — and cooped up further down still, beneath the blank and blur you heard when you sought some received indigenous meaning — listening all the way down, you began to overhear the lives of millions of men and women who went their particular ways here, whose roots and legacy come together in the cities we live in. Halifax, Montreal, Toronto, Vancouver: "city" meant something still unspoken, but rampant with energy. Hearing it was like watching the contours of an unexpected continent declare themselves through the familiar lawns and faces of your block.

Though that again is hindsight. You heard an energy, and those lives were part of it. Under the surface alienation of our words, and beneath the deeper muteness, there was a living barrage of meaning. Private, civil, religious — unclassifiable finally, but teeming to be uttered. I felt that press of meaning; I had no idea what it was, but I could sense it swarming toward words.

And buoyed by that energy, I started to write again — revising and expanding *Civil Elegies*.

◆

Why does this tale of writing, falling silent for three years, beginning to write again, feel slightly foreign?

Because I barely recognize the protagonist, for one thing. The story implies a ten-year certainty of purpose — which I admire as I read. But what I actually felt during most of that decade was beleaguered drifting. And while it was punctuated with flashes of clarity, I'm mortified to report that the flashes were often at odds with each other.

Moreover, the chronology is awkward, uncooperative. The story implies a sequence that runs like this: poet writes artificial early work; dissatisfied with its stiffness, he stops writing; George Grant's essays furnish an explanation for his block; as a result something called "cadence" happens to him, and he starts to write in a new and freer way.

That's easy to follow, and edifying. But in fact it went more like this. Poet writes artificial early work, while being haunted by a deeper music; after his first book appears, he connects with "cadence"; meanwhile he's reading George Grant in dribs & drabs; for no discernible reason, he stops being able to write when the second book comes out; three years later, again with no obvious cause, he returns to that book and makes it multi-vocal.

How does it all fit together? There are so many loose ends, I've given up looking for a sequential logic; none of the causes and effects are in the right place. But even a thematic account of the process, which is what I've sketched here, dramatizes and streamlines things that were much more tangled, murky, and banal when they occurred.

◆

Those are reservations that need to be recognized. But they matter less than the underlying experience that generated them.

One thing I find now is that I can write only from the promptings of cadence. I can no more observe something in the street and go write it up than I can fly. Not, at least, if I'm looking for words that resonate.

So it will not do to ignore our halting tongues, and blithely report on surface things — as if we could will ourselves to be everything we're not. The impasse of writing that is problematic to itself is transcended only when the impasse enters the voice and subject matter; when writing accepts and names its own condition as it names the world. Any other course (except in deliberately minor work) leads to writing whose joints and musculature don't work together.

To name your colonial condition is not necessarily to assign explicit terms to it. It may be spelled out on the page, as in the poetry of Milton Acorn or Gaston Miron. But the weight of the silence can also be conveyed by the sheer pressure behind the words that finally break it. Then to name one's condition is to recreate the halt and stammer, the wry self-deprecation, the rush of celebratory élan and the vastness of the still unspoken surround in which a colonial writer first comes to know *his* house, *his* father, *her* city and land — encounters them in their own unuttered terms, and finds words being born to speak them. I think of Al Purdy's poems. Beneath the words our absentee masters have given us, there is an undermining silence. It saps our nerve. And beneath that silence, there is a raw welter of cadence that tumbles and strains toward words. It makes the silence a blessing, because it shushes easy speech. That cadence is home.

We do not own cadence. And it's not in Canada; Canada is in it, along with everything else. Nor is it real only for colonials. But it has its own way of speaking our lives, if we are willing to be struck dumb.

Through us, it seeks to issue in the articulate gestures of being here.

3. Silence

WHAT ARE THESE "ARTICULATE GESTURES" OF CADENCE? I believe they depend on silence — perhaps a deeper silence than we've spoken of so far.

There's a moment when I experience other people, situations, things as standing forth with a clarity that make me want to weep and to celebrate physically at the same time. It's the moment when something becomes overwhelmingly real in two lights at once. An old person, whose forward thrust to go on living and whose mortality reach me at the same instant. A child who is coursed through with the lovely energies of its body, and yet is totally vulnerable before the coming decades of its life. A social movement, charged with a passion for decent lives, and at the same time with the egoism and venality that will destroy it. A table, at once a well-worn companion and a disregarded adjunct. Each stands forth as what it is most fully, and most preciously, because the emptiness in which it rests declares itself so overpoweringly. We realize that this thing or person, this phrase, this event *need not be*. And at that moment, it reveals its vivacious being as though it had just begun to exist.

The recognition is subjective, I suppose; it is *our* perception that changes. But the double situation of the child, the table, the social movement is already a given; its life and its death are simultaneous, whether we recognize it or not. The fact that we can be open to it only sporadically doesn't change this coinciding of what-is with its own nonbeing. And at those privileged moments, the table, the child, the grandparent stand fast and also come toward us, saying, "Utter me. Write me. Tell my story."

Thus it is in meeting the emptiness with which living particulars are shot through — their mortality, their corruption; and in a colony, their wordlessness — that we can cherish them most fully as what they are. Until that time, we may have cared for them only as things we could possess or use. But in this luminous, perishable aspect, they assume their own being for us.

To accept nonbeing at home in what-is, to accept what-is at home in nonbeing, is perhaps the essential act of being human.

And what-is makes its mortal being known to us in cadence. *That* is what I started to hear. In the vibrant rhythms of cadence, each thing declares, not only what it is, nor even how it is — but *that* it is. At all. Thus each thing comes to resound in its own silence.

The inauthenticity of our public space is only one such grounding; I am certain the silence I go into is more than civil. But to write in colonial space is to have that silence laid upon you. Whatever else overtakes you, the world you move in and the words you use are already cankered with it. When they come alive in cadence, they come alive in it.

◆

There's one more thing. The mystique of void is seductive, as I know to my cost. Yet nobody sane will give thanks for what is evil, nor for what keeps scotching vulnerable lovely things without remorse. They can't just be slotted into some lofty scheme of things, handy aids to ontological contemplation. Evil and innocent suffering — to recognize that they teem at the heart of being is not to say that they're comfy, or good, or even acceptable. They're an open wound.

That granted, your first response to things that strike at life and goodness undergoes a change, when you discern that everything is most fully itself in the presence of its own emptiness. I cannot say more about that change, however, since I do not understand it very far.

◆

A poem enacts in words the presence of what we live among. It arises from the tough, delicate, heartbreaking rooting of what-is in its own nonbeing. From that rooting, there arise elemental movements of being: of hunger, of play, of rage, of celebration, of dying. Such movements are always particular, speaking the things which are. A poem enacts those movements in words.

Quick in its own silence, cadence seeks to issue in the articulate gestures of being here.

Roots and Play

I wrote this piece in 1975, for a conference on children's literature. But it started gestating ten years earlier, during bedtime readings for two small girls.

Since that time, I'd been making my way as an adult poet. But I loved the way my daughters had connected with Mother Goose. *So I tried my hand at nursery rhymes, and a slim manuscript took shape — growing to a fat manuscript — growing to a mini-behemoth. It was still growing when Hugh Kane, the major-domo at Macmillan, took a chance on publishing it. And so* Alligator Pie *(for youngsters) and* Nicholas Knock and Other People *(for not-so-youngsters) came out together in September, 1974.*

What ensued was never formally planned: a frenetic national tour, cobbled together on the fly as it gathered momentum. Here I was, a solitary egghead poetical hermit, zigzagging across Canada for three months — giving readings, some of them to hundreds of children, up to six times a day. Bookstores ran out of Alligator Pie. *So did the Macmillan warehouse. Twice.*

And now, a year later, I was at this conference, pondering what had happened. Not the media hullabaloo, which had subsided by then. But the pith and gist of children's poetry, which I had rediscovered while reading nursery rhymes to my daughters, ten years before.

Alligator pie, alligator pie,
If I don't get some, I think I'm gonna die.
Give away the green grass, give away the sky,
But don't give away my alligator pie.

1. Writing as an Adult Children

ONE DAY, IN THE SPRING OF 1966, I WAS HEADING OUT ON MY bike to get some milk. And as the pedals went around, a meaningless phrase started repeating in my mind — "*Al*-li-*ga*-tor *pie* ... *al*-li-*ga*-tor *pie* ..." — in time with the pedals. The words had appeared out of nowhere, and soon other bits and pieces were chiming in too: "*Al*-li-*ga*-tor *stew*" ... "I *don't* know *what* I'll *do* ..." I couldn't make them stop. So I turned around, rode home, and scribbled down all the bits I could remember. Then I headed out to the store, and bought some milk.

Truth be told, I just wanted to get the fool thing out of my head. I'd started making up nursery rhymes for my daughters — but this was clearly not one of the keepers. I had no inkling that, over the next few decades, children around the world would take possession of it.

◆

Mind you, that had started before any of the rhymes were published. I finished the alligator poem, despite my initial resistance. And whenever I read to kids, that was the one they came away skipping to and chanting.

So I had to accept: the voice on the bike knew better than I did. And over time, that changed my sense of what I was up to. I wasn't writing poems *for* children — not if they had staying power. I was writing poems *as* children. And that was a whole different gig. Because, like most healthy adults, I have a batch of youngsters still resident in my nervous system. Persistent, like growth rings on a tree. And the key to writing, I realized, was to connect with one of those children, and go wherever its instincts led.

On the other hand, if I relied on my grown-up notions of what children like, I would crank out something lame and condescending — pasted onto the child's life from the outside.

◆

But that's only half the story. It's true, I need an inner child to take the lead. But once it does, I won't surrender my prerogative as a grown-up poet. The craft is up to me.

So the thing has to be well written. Whether it's casual or classy, a children's poem has to clear its own hurdles with grace. It may be simple, but simplicity can be harder to achieve than complexity. And while its way of experiencing things may be a five-year-old's, I can't accept that a poem should play fast and loose with that experience — recreate it in a slipshod or patronizing way. ("C'mon, it's only kidlit.")

Nor is it just a matter of craft. There's a whole rosy-eyed view of childhood which sometimes infects children's literature. It makes me wonder whether people who promote it have spent any time with real kids; they seem to be seeking a safe and gauzy childhood that never was. I've written a few poems to skewer that hankering.

Suzy grew a moustache,
  A moustache,
  A moustache,
Suzy grew a moustache,
  And Polly grew a beard.

Suzy looked peculiar,
  Peculiar,
  Peculiar,
Suzy looked peculiar,
  And Polly looked weird.

Suzy got the garden-shears,
    Garden-shears,
    The garden-shears,
Suzy got the garden-shears
    And Polly got a bomb.

Now Suzy's face is smooth again,
    Smooth again,
    Smooth again,
Suzy's face is smooth again,
    And Polly's face is gone.

What I really want from a book of poems is that it be a birthday party, to which all our selves are invited. There has to be room for aggression, anxiety, bratty humour — not too much, but enough. And then I welcome intimate feelings too, and the thrill of a new friend, and those wordless hunches when we sense a world that is home for a spell:

Columbine is sweet,
And sweet alyssum blooming —
Tell me who you love,
And I'll whisper what I'm dreaming. ...

◆

And if the two do come together — the child's impulses, and the adult's craft — there can arise a simplicity which occasionally appears on the yonder side of complexity.

I came to that first with children's verse. My adult poetry often traces the way our daily particulars jangle against each other. But until I started writing children's poetry, I was pretty much mired in the jangle. I could seldom find a way to release the lyric sense, that things are sounding for once in the same key. Such a unity may be joyous or downcast, scary or zany. But for a brief time it holds, and the world coheres.

This one-ing of the world is the essence of lyricism. What makes a lyric ring true is not just lullaby rhythms or mellifluous sounds, but the intuition of a coherence of being. That makes a single, singing self possible again — or at least glimpsable.

Silverly,
    Silverly,
Over the
    Trees
The moon drifts
    By on a
Runaway
    Breeze.

Dozily,
    Dozily,
Deep in her
    Bed,
A little girl
    Dreams with the
Moon in her
    Head.

I don't claim that the lyrical is superior to the meditative. Nor vice versa. Indeed, I won't be content till I can do both in the same poem. But it was only when yesterday's children and today's adult started writing together that I could get close to the lyric at all.

2. Roots

What kindles your imagination when you write as an adult children? I can't speak for other poets, but I know two things that have kindled mine: *roots*, and *play*.

There's a shock of recognition that lies in wait in books, which readers in English Canada discovered when our homegrown literature took off in the 1960s. It's so basic, you may find it remarkable that we took so long to get here. All I can say is, we find it remarkable too.

It's the discovery that excellent writing is rooted in its own time and place — and *they can be your own*. The realization doesn't come in these abstract terms, of course. It arises when you read a book by a contemporary, and find it speaking *your* place, *your* time, *your* ways of being — catching the inflections of how they are more truly than you ever thought possible. Suddenly the book is alive inside your life: very daring, very inevitable, very much just *there*, like a new intimacy you didn't know about till it happened, but already you're at home.

This confirmation of what we are, I call "roots." The kind of book I'm talking about is rooted in its own locale, of course. But the book in turn affords roots to the reader. Which means, it makes the texture of their everyday life palpable, raises it to imaginative visibility. It's a kind of psychic second nesting.

◆

About 1965, as I was beginning to read *Mother Goose* to my first daughter, these thoughts were tumbling around in my head. And I found myself starting to chafe. In one way, my thoughts seemed ludicrous. But in another way, I had no choice.

What I was thinking was this. "Here's a little girl, not yet two, and she's getting bounced to the rhythm of pipers and pence, of curds and whey, of piglets and pease porridge hot — and she hasn't the foggiest notion what they are. For shame! Thought control! *Mother Goose* is a tool of British imperialism!"

But that seemed silly — if only because, had she been getting bounced to the rhythm of hockey sticks and T4 slips and dominion-provincial conferences, she wouldn't have known what *they* were either. And I didn't want to deprive her of *Mother Goose*. Was the argument taking me in a doctrinaire, book-banning direction? ... No thank you.

"Still," I went on, "isn't it bizarre that, before she's two, this child is learning what Canadians know by heart: that the imagination always leads to the kingdom of elsewhere?" Finally, I arrived at a realization which struck me with the full force of its obviousness, and yet felt almost illicit, since I had never heard it spoken out loud.

The nursery rhymes I love, and my children love, are exotic to us. (I still don't know what a tuffet is, and in a perverse way I hope I never find out.) But they were in no way exotic to the people who first spoke them. "Three little pigs went to market": that once had the everyday immediacy of — of what? "Three wiener dogs went to Loblaws," something like that. The air of faraway charm and simpler pastoral existence which now suffuses *Mother Goose* was in no way part of those rhymes' initial appeal. I don't want to wish away that aura; it's part of their enduring in time. But the people who told those rhymes for centuries would be boggled if they could experience them the way children do now — as a collection of things they've never seen, places they've never heard of, in words they will often meet only in those verses. The rhymes themselves haven't changed. But the world around them has. So where they once confirmed their listeners' roots, articulated "home" in the earliest season of their lives, they no longer do.

To claim that gift today, I realized, we have to look somewhere else: in our own backyards. Which is what I set out to do.

◆

The readiest thing was to play with the place names that dot the country. The Indigenous names in particular have an incantatory lilt. Here's a rhyme that simply hunkers into their music:

If I lived in Temagami,
Temiskaming, Kenagami,
Or Lynx, or Michipicoten Sound,
I wouldn't stir the whole year round

Unless I went to spend the day
At Bawk, or Nottawasaga Bay.
Or Missinabi, Moosonee,
Or Kahshe or Chicoutimi.

Mind you, a lot of the things I tried in the map-reading mode were pretty pedestrian; they had nothing going for them but their programmatic intent, and I ditched them. Gradually I realized that the externals didn't have to be so self-conscious. If it felt right to include something explicitly Canadian, fine; if it didn't feel right, equally fine. There was a mounting sense of excitement as I relinquished the more crusading aspects of the thing, and discovered there really *was* a music in the lives of the children I know and am. There was no need to *give* a poem roots; if you just sat still, letting things find their way into you, they would be happy to come as themselves, and sometimes be poems. It gave me a sense of almost physical release as places, things, experiences, even individual words, which as far as I knew had never been set vibrating in poems, found their way into these verses.

Skyscraper, skyscraper,
Scrape me some sky:
Tickle the sun
While the stars go by.

Tickle the stars
While the sun's climbing high,
Then skyscraper, skyscraper
Scrape me some sky.

◆

One poem from that time shows how far the question of roots had come. I'd grown fascinated with a love affair my son was carrying on. But to coax it into words would be tricky, since he was only two. The challenge had nothing to do with contemporary references (apart from daycare), and everything to do with the inflections of a child's inner life. Catching those inflections could afford a subtler, more inward kind of rooting.

I've got a Special Person
At my daycare, where I'm in.
Her name is Mrs. Something
But we mostly call her Lynn.

'Cause Lynn's the one that shows you
How to squish a paper cup.
And Lynn's the one that smells good
When you make her pick you up.
(She smells good when she picks you up.)

She knows a lot of stories
And she reads them off by heart.
There's one about a bear, but I
Forget the other part.

She bit me on my knee once, 'cause I
Said she couldn't scream,
And then I sent her in the hall,
And then we had ice cream.

I guess I'm going to marry Lynn
When I get three or four,
And Lynn can have my crib, or else
She'll maybe sleep next door.

'Cause Martin wants to marry Lynn
And live here too, he said.
(I guess he'll have to come, but he's
Too little for a bed.)

By this point, the quest for roots had virtually dissolved as a conscious pursuit. If a poem could utter its locale by its inflections as much as its content, the search did not depend on externals of time and place. It depended on writing that rang true.

3. Play

Coming out of a WASP tradition, I realized in my twenties that I was emotionally constricted. There were feelings I didn't have access to, though I could sense their pent-up power. Or if I did connect with them, I couldn't express them in daily life. Or if they came out there, I still couldn't channel them in poems. What I craved was the chance to *play* — to unleash this buried life in a kind of freed-up rehearsal and wooing.

And that too led me to write as an adult children. For the task of children *is* to play, and thereby explore the lives they will later live. Their play may be trivial or profound, celebratory or cruel; in fact, such breadth is a characteristic of children's play. It ranges from the simple release of energy to solemn rituals of loss and celebration, enacting a gamut of possible selves in the safe house of let's-pretend. As Johan Huizinga says in *Homo Ludens*, "Frivolity and ecstasy are the twin poles between which play moves."

So my children's work unfurled new gestures of being human. "New," not in the sense that no one had ever used these emotional muscles before. But new in the sense of breaking taboos: against goofiness, anger, rejoicing, bodily grace — whatever energies had been tamped down in my culture. Enacting those impulses on the page *was* the play I'm speaking of.

◆

Let me start with some poems I wrote for older children; they're found in *Nicholas Knock and Other People*. Many, I see now, approached the challenge of play as their undeclared theme. Often they brought some tight-assed speaker or character into collision with a vibrant, larger-than-life personage. The effect was to pose the question, "What are you going to do about *this*? Can you handle such unbridled vitality?" And the response was different each time, since I had no fixed answer.

Here's a stanza from the earliest piece, "The Cyclone Visitors":

> Rasputin the Monk
> Is dancing, dead drunk,
> On the top of the New City Hall.
> I've called for a cop.
> I've begged him to stop,
> But he will not stop dancing at all —
> The gall!
> If he doesn't stop dancing, he'll fall.
> You can't *dance* on a New City Hall!

There are three vignettes in the poem, and each explores the same possibility — that the bawdy, the holy, the untameably vital might remain off-limits for keeps. The purse-lipped speaker is clearly not taking any chances with zanies like this. And that's where I started — imagining the worst.

In *Nicholas Knock*, there's a range of these encounters. In the title poem, the emissary of larger life is the silver honkabeest, whose intermittent presence haunts young Nicholas, and spurs him to confront the forces of conformity:

> Frisky, most silver, serene —
> bright step at the margins of air, you
> tiny colossus and

winsome and
master me, easy in sunlight, you
gracious one come to me, live in
my life.

◆

But the poems for young children take a different tack. They're not *about* "the challenge of play." They simply *play*. Often that's all they do. And they play at such an elemental level — the level of vowels and consonants — that it's hard to articulate what's going on.

How do you discuss sheer play in poetry? I don't know any established approach. In fact, I'm not sure we have a language for talking about it at all. Here's a false lead, which we can mention and then rule out. When people try to pin down the nature of play in my poetry, they often call it "nonsense." But that term is better reserved for something quite different: for poetry that weaves together logic and irrationality, and in the process demolishes many of our assumptions about how the world works. In this specialized sense of the term, Lewis Carroll is the master of nonsense.

He thought he saw an Elephant
That practised on a fife:
He looked again, and found it was
A letter from his wife.
"At length I realise," he said,
"The bitterness of Life!" ...

He thought he saw an Argument
That proved he was the Pope:
He looked again, and found it was
A Bar of Mottled Soap.
"A fact so dread," he faintly said,
"Extinguishes all hope!" ...

Now, that is true non-sense: an elegant rehearsal of logical discourse, in a world where logic fails to apply. And I would be honoured to write in that company. But the fact is, it's not my primary bent. What people speak of as "nonsense" in my work is something different.

I want to call it "play." But that creates a problem of terminology. If I resort to the word here, I need to distinguish what I mean from our earlier usage. "Children's play" took in the whole gamut of let's-pretend: strutting around as the king of the castle; burying a deceased insect; caring for dolls; shooting somebody dead. We've already looked at that broad sense of the term. But now I want to apply it to a narrower band on the spectrum — to kibitzing, high spirits, release of animal energy. And what I want to know is this: when a poem plays, in the sense of sheer exuberance, what does that play consist of?

When I ponder the question, it leads me back to *Mother Goose*.

◆

What boggles me in nursery rhymes is the way they rely on the absolute basics: raw sound and rhythm. That's as close to pure music as poetry can get. And for the poet, it means there's nowhere to hide. Not stories; not images; not bright ideas. Either the thing works at this primal level, or it doesn't work at all.

Consider a consummate eleven-word poem:

> Jack be nimble,
> Jack be quick,
> Jack jump over
> The candlestick.

I don't know how many times I've repeated that rhyme, trying to figure out what makes it work. You'll follow where we're going most readily if you try it yourself. Say the verse out loud several times; slow it down to half-speed; exaggerate the stressed syllables. You'll feel it take on the force of a chant or incantation.

Now, try changing a few of the words, without altering the meaning. Put in words with different sounds:

> Jack be speedy,
> Jack be quick,
> Jack hop over
> The candlestick.

Or put in words that change the rhythm:

> Jack be fast,
> Jack be quick,
> Jack hurdle over
> The candlestick.

Can you feel how the little mantra goes askew, stops enacting its moves with such poise? When the syllabic play doesn't click, we can sense it in our muscles. And if you go back to the original, you'll feel even more clearly how right it is. But what *makes* it right?

Whatever it is, it's nothing that scholarship can reveal. Iona and Peter Opie tell us the rhyme probably derives from the game of candle-leaping, which was practised for centuries in England. You put a lighted candle on the floor, and tried to jump over it without extinguishing the flame. If you succeeded, you had good luck for a year.

But while that provides some engaging background, it gets us no closer to understanding the poem's play.

◆

Since I mess around with words, my inclination is to look somewhere else. Namely, to the soundscape of the poem: the kinetic shape which the sounds and the stresses create. But the point is not just to show that such a shape exists. Read any four lines from the telephone book, and you'll hear a pattern of one kind or another in the sounds. So what? The question is, what does the sound pattern accomplish? What story is being told in the auditory and kinesthetic dimension of the poem?

Let's find out. Translating the elusive music into words can take a disproportionate, almost risible amount of space. But that comes with the territory. We understand these things by body knowledge first. And when we translate it into head knowledge, we're displacing it from its native habitat. Please bear with the drawn-out translation that follows.

"Jack Be Nimble" is about a game. Even if we've never heard of candle-leaping, it's clear that Jack is being urged to show his mettle with a mighty leap. That is: the *subject* of the poem is play.

But while "play" is a key concept in our discussion, it doesn't help to pin that label on the content. Not because it doesn't apply, but because the content is not what makes the words skip and soar in the first place. We saw that when we substituted "speedy" for "nimble," "hurdle" for "jump." The content was still "play" — but the poem no longer played. Or not with the same grace and verve.

Let's try again.

Not only is "Jack Be Nimble" about a game — it acts out the stages *in* the game. The poem is a starter's command, which follows the general form: "On your mark — get set — GO!" It could have read, "Be nimble — be quick — JUMP!" The poem gives us Jack's preparatory tensing, in lines one and two; and then, stretching across lines three and four, the jump itself.

With that in mind, consider the poem first as a tissue of *sound*. And we'll go right down to the granular level — to individual syllables. You'll notice there are two stressed syllables in each line. The first line, for instance, goes, "*Jack* be / *nim*-ble." And if you listen to the syllables you naturally emphasize, you'll hear, "a ... ih" (in "*Jack*" and "*nim-*").

Now, let's follow the shape of the sounds which the stressed syllables create. They run:

a ... ih (Jack ... nim-)
a ... ih (Jack ... quick)
a ... oh (Jack ... o-)
a ... ih (Can- ... -stick)

But this is striking. The poem departs from the basic pattern ("a ... ih") only once — changing to "a ... oh" as Jack is achieving liftoff. And then it returns to the original pattern ("a ... ih") as he returns to the floor. In a way that's almost too subtle to articulate, the vowel music of the poem is acting out its own content; the action unfolds right in the sound of the words. (Which is why "Jack be speedy" was a dud; it sabotaged the sound pattern before it began.)

Are we conscious of all this when we read the rhyme? I never was, though I felt it clearly enough. Did whoever wrote "Jack Be Nimble" set out to create this effect? I have no way of knowing, but I bet they didn't. I bet they lucked into it. At most, I bet they kept on playing with the words until they felt right — meaning, until the sounds gave the kind of subliminal satisfaction we've teased into daylight. Perhaps it happened as the rhyme was reshaped over generations, till it stabilized in this form.

However it came about, the result is a verse we can't get out of our heads, our bodies even. And the reason for that is the rococo aplomb of the soundscape, which is both shapely in itself, and a live enactment of the poem's meaning.

◆

We've considered the pattern of *sounds* in "Jack Be Nimble." And something similar is true in the *rhythm* as well. Read the verse out loud again — this time, concentrating on the lighter and stronger stresses.

The basic rhythmic unit is familiar: a strong beat followed by a weak beat. A trochee, in metrical terminology. And each line consists of two trochees — though with a couple of key departures. The first line sets up the pattern unmistakably: "**Jack** be /**nim**-ble." The second line is the same, except it does what an English speaker's ear expects — it drops the final weak syllable. So we hear it as a silent rest: "**Jack** be / **quick** [__]."

But notice what happens next: there are a couple of departures from that rhythmic pattern. The third line begins with a spondee — that is, with *two* stressed syllables, *two* strong beats: "**Jack jump.**" Pronouncing these two heavy stresses slows the line down — perhaps to the extent of a tiny pause between "Jack" and "jump," as our tongue makes its way through the viscous consonants. (I also hear a lengthening of the "J" in "Jack," though I wouldn't press the point.) All this configures the dynamics of the poem in a subtle but unmistakable way. And it's not gratuitous that this slower rhythm occurs where it does. This is where Jack is getting set, digging in for the leap. (Which is why "hurdle" didn't work; it made the rhythm contradict that getting-set moment.)

The other departure comes in the final line. There's an extra weak syllable at the beginning — the word "the." It's a grace note, which gives the rhythm an added skip. ... You can finish the case yourself. The extra syllable lengthens the duration of the leap, mimes Jack's time in the air. And when the first strong stress of the fourth line explodes in "**can-**" — which we're likely to say with the strongest stress and the highest pitch of any syllable in the poem — we feel an adrenalin boost, as Jack soars over the flame.

On its tiny scale, "Jack Be Nimble" works beautifully. It takes an absurd number of words to describe what transpires in the soundscape. But in our bodies, we register its shape at once. It's the shape of a leap — the shape of a *yes*! of triumph. And if we want to take part in the poem's play, it's in this sonic/kinesthetic dimension that we find it unfolding.

I suspect that every nursery rhyme we carry around with us, imprinted in memory at the cellular level, is unforgettable precisely because its play unfolds with shapely panache in that dimension. Not like "Jack Be Nimble" — but like itself.

◆

Where does this get us?

A good nursery rhyme is an *incantation*. The sheer sound and rhythm enact a spell of some kind — one that meshes both with the way our muscles want to move, and with some primal intuition of how the world fits together and flows.

This helps explain a striking feature of nursery rhymes. Consider how many start with a line of pure sound, virtually uncontaminated by meaning:

> Hickory, dickory, dock ...
>
> Handy, spandy, Jack-a-Dandy ...
>
> Peter, Peter, pumpkin eater ...

It's a magic spell, ushering us into a parallel world of the imagination. Only after the spell has been cast in the first line do the sounds distil into sense. And the play can proceed.

Or that is my hunch. But you can't verify it by looking at a nursery rhyme on the page; it will simply look back at you. That's like trying to enjoy a piece of music by reading the score. You have to have a very young child on your knee. And you have to *do* the poem with her — very slowly, with a certain gleeful verve. Let each syllable arrive like a new day in your life. Then a rhyme comes something like a birthday, and a quickening in the rhythm like a new season.

These similes are not idle. It really is possible with a good nursery rhyme to experience the incantation this way. Rhythm in the words, translated via the bounce of your knee to the child's bum, and then up her spine. Sounds that open out like parasols, a succession of colours, almost meaning something but mainly filling your field of attention one after the other, and sometimes sliding back on themselves when the same sound rhymes. Because the medium of nursery rhymes is oral and communal, you encounter these constituents as an environment. One which triggers the old rhythms of cyclical delight: stability, and the excursions of novelty. And you can feel those instincts stirring inside you, if you help the child give you permission.

This may sound like mystification. It isn't. I experience it all the time in nursery rhymes — though the words I'm using to describe it are provisional. Nor do I know *how* you find rhythms and sounds that cast a spell, enact an incantation. All I do is play around with words until they work.

And that leaves me with renewed admiration for the anonymous masters of *Mother Goose*. Because what looks simple, simple-minded even — to plunk down a bunch of words, and make children laugh and skip to them — is much, much harder than it seems. It's undeniable that some rhymes sink into their imaginations, their bodies almost, like water into a sponge. While others remain clever, inert little exercises, which never come home to a single child. But there's seldom an obvious explanation why it's one or the other. Either you get it right, or the poem goes belly up.

When you set out to play directly in words, you're like a jazz musician doing improv. There's no safety net.

◆

Where do these ruminations lead?

It may be of interest to know that one children's poet was propelled by a craving for roots, and a need to play. But once you sit down to read a poem, that falls away. The only thing that matters is whether the poem lives and breathes.

Nor does it give me any clue about what to write next. I'm pleased with these poems, but like most writers I revolve around the things I haven't written yet. And when I look back at my children's books from that perspective, I'm anything but satisfied.

Not because of what's in them, but because of what *isn't*. I spent so much energy just clearing a path toward rooted play, and so little time making its poems. And I think: there are terrors, and joys, and states of daily despair and amazement that I was barely making a pass at. How could I take this as anything but a first flirtation — trying to pass off mischievousness as bawdy vitality, and a timid sense of discomfort as holy terror?

Then I read the poems with children again, and they do trigger the things I was reaching for. And I no longer know what to think. Finally I let them go, and turn back to the poems still buzzing to be written. They are what compels me, though I know that once they're safe in words they too will slide away, leaving me confused, exultant, still in wait for the cranky miracle.

Polyphony:
Enacting a Meditation

At the time I wrote "Polyphony," a certain type of poem was widely admired. It was witty and skilled, replete with meaningful symbols and knowing pronouncements — all presented in traditional poetic forms. It was Auden Lite, and I thought it sucked.

But it gave me something to push against. I'd been writing a very different kind of poetry, finding my way by trial and error. Now I wanted to clarify and consolidate the moves I'd been making intuitively. *And one key to that was* polyphony.

But how does polyphony actually work, when you're navigating it line by line? I didn't talk about that in the essay — not with specific examples. However, in my essay on Al Purdy there's a close reading of his "Love at Roblin Lake" (105-8), which examines the way a master handles it.

1.

I WANT TO EXPLORE THE WAYS IN WHICH A MEDITATIVE POEM *means*.

I take a "meditative poem" to be a ruminative poem of some length, which moves from one state of affairs at the beginning to a different state at the end. The trajectory proceeds in stages — as a quest on the speaker's part.

◆

What a meditation means isn't limited to what it says — its paraphrasable content. The meaning also depends on *how* things are said. On the poem's voice — its rhythms and tonations.

2.

The voice of a poem *embodies* one or more of the timbres which animate things.

To read a poem properly is to participate in its vocal journey.

3.

Most poems are monophonic; they're written in a single voice.

And the most common single voice in contemporary poetry is the one that *states*. Along the lines of, "When I think of how you betrayed me, I feel angry."

What does that voice embody? A discursive equanimity, which reports on its feelings — and everything else — from a safe distance. But the feelings themselves have no reality in the poem. They never dislodge the declarative tone, never find a voice of their own.

Despite the speaker's assertion, such a poem doesn't "feel angry" any more than it feels pink. The voice gives the lie to its own utterance.

◆

If the poem wants to ring true, let it canvass the details of the betrayal — and canvass them *angrily*.

Anger need not be mentioned by name. But it has to be embodied in the movement & texture & pitch of the speaker's words. As a for-instance: "You rat! You scum! You *betrayed* me." Now the speaker is no longer making calm remarks about his supposèd anger — he's sputtering with rage.

◆

This approach — of embodying the speaker's anger — demands considerable vocal finesse. As do inflections of coltishness, ecstasy, musing, despair. It's a technical challenge, and it calls for savvy technical solutions — using line breaks, levels of diction, interweaving of imagery and —

Just a minute, Mr. Lee. What have you got against a calm and reasonable tone of voice?

Nothing at all — so long as it doesn't hog the mic.

The discursive voice embodies one legitimate strain in our makeup — a detached observer's. But if that's the only voice we hear, it excludes all the other currents in the speaker. And it's not just the speaker who gets straitened; other people and trees and wars and daily events all get un-selved by a vocal range that can't accommodate their music. The whole world gets shrunk down to a single, reportorial bandwidth. Anything deeper, more epochally alive, gets minified.

Hmmm. ... Perhaps.

4.

If a monophonic poem has a different voice than the discursive — *any* different voice — it's already a signal achievement.

But what makes a poem univocal is not a particular voice. It's the fact that the voice is prolonged throughout the poem.

This monophony isn't always a bad thing. A short poem might fly apart, if it tried to incorporate three voices in ten lines. The poem may need to be in a single tone.

But monophonic poetry is not our main concern. Let's move on.

5.

Most readers can read monophonically. Most poets oblige.

But a poem can be *polyphonic*. Its voice can change five times in thirty lines; it can rage, state, noodle, cavort, then shudder with grief.

Polyphony in writing is the art of orchestrating successive voices across a work.

◆

Poly-phony. Many sounds: many voices.

But polyphony takes different forms in different disciplines. Polyphonic music presents two or more melodic lines at the same time — using multiple singers, or multiple instruments.

But because it exists on the page, polyphonic poetry works differently. It presents one voice *after* another; the voices enter consecutively, rather than simultaneously. (There are rare exceptions — such as the works for simultaneous speakers by Glenn Gould and Robert Bringhurst. But they remain outliers.)

6.

So voice *embodies*. And polyphony *enacts*.

For it to be a meditation at all, a poem must embody in voice the way its experience is initially focused — and then proceed to envoice another focusing, and then another. To live its way to deeper and more complete knowing, which is what a meditation does, it has to vocally enact the stages of its quest.

◆

The trajectory of a meditation consists of this movement from inflection to inflection. The clash and resonance of timbres. Or to put it differently: the changing inflections are the *plot* of the meditation.

Otherwise, it hasn't budged an inch. Be it a lament, a thesis, a tirade, there's no story being told.

7.

To write polyphonically is to contest poetry as it's now written. Maybe to repudiate it altogether. To walk off that field, and look for the real one.

8.

Sometimes one inflection will hold for twenty lines; at other times, there may be three changes in the same space. With voices flickering or criss-cross or interlaced. Till there are scores of tonalities in the piece, kinetic, and the whole thing starts to sing across within itself.

That's part of what I mean. It's a start. It still isn't there.

9.

To read a meditation rightly is a matter of hearing its shorter and longer vocal rhythms at the same time. The way you hear successive movements in a symphony: absorbing the local passages, and simultaneously discerning the larger progression from one to the next.

This vocal trajectory provides the through-line.

◆

But it doesn't follow a fixed itinerary, like checking in at pre-established points on a route map.

The poem has to live its way through a course of attending — and be changed by what it encounters. The changes might carry it anywhere. The guide is what rings true in the voice.

◆

So it's not as if you have a kit of portable styles, which you slather over whatever new content comes along. The voice gets generated — often for the first & only time — by the torque and tension of each new place you come to. You may spend days or weeks, months even, finding how to utter the five-line place you've entered. You first occupy it when you hit on the voice that rings true for *this* moment of consciousness, focused by *this* burden of content.

10.

This means, the poem has to be open. Open in its layout on the page: open to going anywhere, in any voice.

◆

And the movements are a series of improvised leaps and recoils. Like body English out loud. They may come in off-key with the one before, and the one before that, but you realize they've got their own right pitch themselves. And then a funny discordant concord starts to orchestrate itself out of the clashes and changes.

Say it's ticking along very quietly, just ticking over, and then all of a sudden it spurts straight up for a bit — ka-*ching!* — till you realize there's a long slow roll coming in from the far side now, it crests right across the spurt and carries the thing out the other side for 20 lines maybe, with just a bit of tremolo around the edges. Bit of titivation. Whatever.

11.

Very pretty. Very poetic. But there's something I don't understand.

When I read an "open" poem — by Pound, say, or Olson — I can't see why anything has to occur where it does. Or even, sometimes, why it has to be in the poem at all. What governs these random leapings-about you described?

Hunches. Trial and error. Hearing the music in your forearms, and trying not to muff it. God knows you spend enough time muffing it, exploring dead ends you have to abandon. You may not have the chops to make it work.

But that doesn't tell us anything. If you start with no pre-established plan, and if content and voice are up for grabs, and you're just winging it, how can you tell when you've muffed it and when you haven't?

What happened to organic form? How can you do anything but set down random bits and pieces, and link them arbitrarily? What does formal coherence even consist *of, in this kind of poem?*

There's something deeper, but I can't get hold of it yet. Something is enforced on you. See, I know my stuff moves around a lot. But I try to make it cohere, by —

12.

You're right. This is phoney.

Phoney? What are you talking about?

It's make-believe. There's nothing here that allows for the emergence of organic form. I haven't said a bleeping word about the source of coherence in polyphonic poetry.

So just cancel it, cancel everything I've said. I've been carrying on as if it was me who creates the tumble and glide on the page. And sure: I write the poem. But I don't *invent* the music I hear; I sit and play in it. Do you think I can boss it around? Most of the time I can't even keep up with it.

And don't you see? Those flexing voices — they're not mine. They're the undermusic. Without it there'd be nothing: no weight, no resonance, just a lot of flailing around. But I've been talking as if you can reduce it all to the technical moves of the writer. That's a piece of modern bafflegab.

I wasn't expecting... Dennis, I'm sorry. But how else could you go at it?

I don't know. But it's not just how you assemble the poem. That's the second step. The primary thing —

13.

There's a swivel and thrum I sense as perpetual — that I hear like a subsonic throbbing, or the sea. I call it "cadence." I connect with it in the way I described in "Cadence, Country, Silence." I was in my twenties, and I got walloped by these whichway energies, teeming in some kind of parallel space. Kinesthetic. Pre-verbal, but itching to issue in words. And *that's* where the poem's coherence comes from.

But cadence, and the mindset of this era — they're not compatible. Cadence is something given, far deeper than my own mind or craft, intimate, other, and which compels my awe. It claims me. But the only language for talking about it is the modern one — the poem as product of technique, the heroic artist fashioning order from the raw material of the world. I don't believe a word of it. But I'm a creature of modernity, and I can't help reverting to the approach it's bred in us.

But that falsifies everything I know at the core. There has to be some way of talking about the two-way traffic between cadence and poem — not just treating the poem as a kind of vocal engineering job.

14.

When I was young, I thought you worked up a frenzy of will and devotion to honour what claimed you. But this is not like that; it's meat-and-potatoes. It's sheer spellbound attending, beneath the threshold of your will. In astonishment, delight, trepidation. In electric fatigue and awe. Knowing you're at home, knowing you may be sullying it, but that's how it is.

◆

The response that cadence evokes is not casual curiosity, nor a desire to possess it, nor to take it apart and see what makes it tick. There's just this active impersonal stillness, and the elemental acknowledgement: cadence *is*, here, perpetual, yes and we're in it. I don't understand what it means, that "cadence is." My head doesn't translate the knowing. But that doesn't bother me. If my mind does its thing with it someday, that's fine. And if not, that's fine too.

If I paid better attention, cadence would be no more real for that.

15.

The source of organic form is cadence. And what needs more room to breathe is the way cadence impinges on you when you're writing.

It begins long before individual words come clear; that's one thing. Before words are any kind of guide to what's getting born.

And cadence *teems.* As a kind of magnetic din, a silent raucous ambient tumult you move around in; very clean though. And always: when you perceive it, when you don't.

What *is* it?

It's *there*, that's all. It's *here.* Not just to sponsor poems. And I know: if you could somehow screen out the literal meaning of words, their polyphony would still enact the gestures of cadence.

Of course, you can't separate the play of vocal inflections from the literal meaning of words. Poetry isn't abstract painting; words denote. But the music does exist at a pre-signifying level. And hearing it properly recapitulates the way the spurt and shimmy and lunge first came at you — which was, they came tumbling through you long before there were words to flesh them out. You were galvanized by cadence, not yet knowing what its rhythmic shape was. Let alone its content.

And what you need, miming that summons, is an utterly supple medium: a voice that can metamorphose from inflection to inflection. Under the press of the necessities of the cadence it's born in. And borne in. Gradually at times; or abruptly, but with no sense of gears being stripped. Nor of it being stage-managed in its changes. Like a field of luminous force, knotted and folding and stalling and skittering back, perpetual live energy. But not rarified, not removed, it's not Ideal; this worries me, almost — does it mean accepting whatever is, good and evil like goulash? Because always it's just there, thudding like something breathing, right now we're in it ... Oink ... *Selah* ...

16.

See, I *know* my stuff moves around. But I go in the straightest line I can. I hate obscurity, I hate gussied-up decoration. There's just the one clean trajectory of attending; you hew to the grain. But in the space of cadence, what people think of as straight lines — standard logical associations, received literary, emotional, even tonal ones — may bear no relation to the actual currents of that space. So if you move in a conventional straight line, you falsify the grain of how things go about being themselves.

17.

It's like the way — to use a limited analogy — it's like the way "straight" lines on the surface of the earth are actually curved. They don't exist in a flat plane to begin with. Suppose you followed a straight, shortest-distance path from Toronto to Barcelona: you'd tunnel through millions of tons of the planet. You wouldn't be following the curve of the surface you live on. But that curvature determines what the shortest distance between two points *is*, on the surface of earth.

And moving with the curvature of earth is what we do every time we take a step. Going in a straight line is an imaginary activity. We don't exist in two dimensions; we were confused for far too long, we thought we lived in Euclid's mind.

18.

But cadential space curves more unpredictably than earth's does. And more than that, it eddies and throbs and hiccups and tumbles and loops. It's not just a matter of recognizing that natural lines of motion curve in three dimensions, rather than extending in two. Because the space of cadence keeps changing its local lines of force. It's like Einsteinian space-time, perpetually tweaked and re-tweaked by the bickering fields of gravity and mass-in-motion.

So the ground rules of direct utterance change too.

For a spell, cadential space may extend monophonically, as though in two dimensions. Then curve off into three. Then it may abruptly pucker, bunch, recoil, explode, go becalmed. You feel out the changing textures as you go.

It's odd to speak of "feeling out" textures, when the poem doesn't exist yet. There's nothing you can point to and say, "*This* is what's guiding me." But the energy of cadence is there; you sense it intuitively, and you put yourself at its behest.

19.

And that's why meditative writing is also a letting-be. You don't just whizz along in the prepackaged grids and grooves we impose on things to organize them. Or if you do you violate, you man-handle, the torque and texture of the space you're writing in. You merely commit a publishable poem; you're a tourist, a small-time imperialist who imports his own right-angle inflections and tries to dig to Barcelona. It makes me claustrophobic.

Mr. Lee, would you mind —

And that's why univocal poetry is so boring, and it feels like vandalism. Even though it may be well-written — a well-written desecration of what is. Most contemporary poetry *is* monophonic. Sure, the content changes. But all you carry away is that single stating voice, buzzing in your ear. And voice embodies being, so you hear the same reductive —

Would you stop ranting about monophonic poetry?!

Right. But I need to make one thing clear. A good monophonic —

Stop. Now. Give it a rest.

20.

Sorry: where were we?

I spoke of a "space" of cadence, and that could imply that the poem is a static map that replicates the space. But it's not. A meditation is the actual *act* of moving through textured space. And the words on the page are the local disturbance — the spoor of its going.

But it's cadence that guides you. And you can feel the heft of the cells in your arms, your neck, your sexual centre — you feel your hopes and forebears straining to reach the articulate gestures of being. You can't compel them. But once you find the flow, once you enter the jostle and hover and rush of the right full carnal gesture in words, there is such a de-kinking, such a sense of deep release into what is quick and still and implacably there, that it nourishes you utterly. And for a time, at least, you can't imagine what other calling makes sense.

21.

It's a paradox.

Polyphony — all these whichway voices — permits a tightly-focused utterance. What's more complex is simpler. Because a shifting tonality lets you hew to the grain, enact the multiform textures of that space — with no detours, no shortcuts, no frills.

22.

There's another thing. I'm stymied when people have trouble hearing polyphony on the page. Often they don't perceive how many shifts there are, how many tonalities are interlaced, till they hear it out loud. They never entered that cadential space in print; for them, the real live poem never started at all.

What were they hearing, I wonder, if they didn't pick up those changes? Is it their ear or my music that was deficient?

23.

I think I know how an open poem coheres. It's because, as the meditation moves through textured space, the changes of voice enact what I've called an articulate gesture of being. A lived coherence.

And that happens because cadential space itself lives through such gestures. When you follow its grain, you find the poem achieving a fundamental movement in its quest. Usually in spite of your preoccupations; sometimes against your will.

So you don't just stitch pieces together. The energies you're miming already enact a basic gesture in the vocabulary of what-is. Like grieving ... or celebrating ... or both at once. Your only job is to trust it.

24.

What is cadence up to?

It comes to me somewhat — though with less of the utter knowing that cadence *is*; whatever it is — you couldn't dissuade me of that short of lobotomizing me — it comes to me sporadically, but then with some measure of that central knowing — it's not just a bright idea; it's the recognition of a fact surfacing beneath your own resources — that what emerges in cadence is the living quick of what-is.

I'm not sure I know what that means. It's a hunch, not a theory. Mostly it seems like something that is so, and whether or not I find out what it means is immaterial.

25.

Is it that the *structure* of what-is is given in the kinetic gestures of cadence? ... That sounds suspect.

Is it some *process* that resounds in cadence?

A process one has gotten tuned into somehow, like a fluke of reception on a shortwave radio.

I think it is. I think it's the process of being. Where "being" is an action verb — like "running" or "shopkeeping." And if my use of the word is obtrusive, I'm sorry. It's not an abstraction; it refers to the most immediate thing there *is* about things. That they are — *at all.* Rather than not being.

It's the workaday miracle, hidden in plain view: that anything *is.*

That's what you sense vibrating in cadence. Ontophony, more than ontology. And you're beholden — beyond provisos or negotiations or alibis.

26.

All my poetry is a response to cadence. Maybe some of the strangeness of what I write will diminish, if a reader perceives that. But it doesn't make the poetry any better or worse to say these things. Indeed, the poetry is almost by the bye; it depends on cadence, but cadence doesn't depend on it.

Which is why I was mortified to speak of polyphony as if it was a matter of vocal engineering. It's something else, as I've tried to show.

Part II

The Poetry of Al Purdy

I first got to know Al Purdy in 1968. I was the (extremely) novice editor at the House of Anansi, then barely a year old. And I'd written to ask if we could reissue his breakthrough collection from 1962, Poems for All the Annettes, *which had gone out of print at Contact Press. He not only agreed, he invited me down to Ameliasburgh to discuss the details.*

So I set out from Toronto, buoyant but anxious. I'd met Purdy a few times, expecting to encounter the same broad range in the man — from corny to pensive to soulful — that I loved in the poetry. But no way. He was backslapping, argumentative, given to bumptious hijinks — and that appeared to be that. The whole inward dimension of the poetry didn't seem to be there; I couldn't even sense him holding it back. Which made me leery. I had some editorial queries on Annettes; *how would this slam-bang, six-pack Purdy react?*

I arrived at noon, and there was some rather laboured horseplay on each side. But when we sat down with the poems, Al's manner changed. He'd been dubious about anyone editing his work, but there were clearly weaker pieces in the book. So we jockeyed ahead with my suggestions; some he scrapped, others he pondered. The best revisions came when he set one of my bright ideas aside, but came back with a far better move to resolve the problem.

What struck me most during that session was his laser-beam focus on the poems — along with a relaxed confidence in his own craft. And it dawned on me: this calm, ferocious concentration gave access to the Purdy-of-many-dimensions I hadn't been able to locate till then. This space of composition was where the dazzling array of voices entered him. And if the sometimes awkward civilian was not in touch with the supple, wide-ranging poet who shared the same skin — so what?

I also remember a goofy little two-step we got into. He had four new poems, written too late to be included in Wild Grape Wine *(which McClelland & Stewart, by now his regular publisher, was bringing out that year). But he wanted to see the poems in a book, and he proposed that we smuggle them into the reprint of* Annettes. *He handed me some typed pages, and hitched his lanky frame back in the chair. One was "House Guest"; another was "At the Quinte Hotel." Two of the classics. They flat-out floored me. But there was a problem, he explained — a serious problem. Jack McClelland would undoubtedly collate the Contact and Anansi editions of* Annettes, *discover that four poems in the reprint were new, and charge Purdy with violating his M&S contract. So to head off this legal disaster, he had prepared a cover story. We would say that "House Guest" and the others were written years ago, but had been accidentally omitted from* Annettes. *We were simply restoring the book to its intended form. ... I promised to vouch for every word of this baloney, and in the poems went.*

Though surprisingly, McClelland never raised the issue at all.

The rest of the visit is a blur. But I remember driving home that night; the car barely needed gas. A wonderful poet was entrusting this landmark book to Anansi. And he'd let me a hair's-breadth into his working space. As I flew along the darkened 401, my whole body was singing. Which it did all the way to T.O. ...

(And eighteen years later, I contributed the following afterword to Purdy's Collected Poems.*)*

In 1944, at a cost of $200, Al Purdy engaged a printer in Vancouver to produce five hundred copies of *The Enchanted Echo*, his first collection of verse. The author was less of an ethereal sprite than the title might imply, being lanky and rawboned in appearance, shambling and somewhat ornery in manner. His debut did not attract widespread attention.

Purdy hailed from United Empire Loyalist country, the region of small towns and rolling farmland at the eastern end of Lake Ontario, where his forebears had settled in the 1780s. He was born there in 1918; his father, a farmer, died two years later. The son grew up in Trenton, in the care of his rigidly religious mother, and left school without completing grade ten. After drifting through occasional jobs, he joined the air force in 1940, and was stationed in British Columbia for the duration of the war.

A less likely bard-in-the-making would be hard to imagine. And the fact is, Purdy would prove to be among the slowest developers in the history of poetry. For decades his progress consisted of false starts and apparently unproductive slogging. Only in retrospect can we discern the sureness of instinct which propelled him through his long apprenticeship, till he emerged as one of the fine poets of our time.

1. The Long Apprenticeship

PURDY HAD BEEN WRITING VERSE SINCE THE AGE OF THIRTEEN, but in complete isolation from the central developments of twentieth-century writing. The modern poets he knew were those in his school anthologies: Kipling and Chesterton and Turner, Carman and Roberts and Pratt. And the poetry he wrote till he was past thirty is exemplified by the title piece from his book:

> Across the autumn flushing streams,
> Adown the misty valleys,
> Atop the skyline's sharp redoubts
> Aswarm with colored alleys —

I caught an echo in my hands,
With pollen mixed for leaven —
I gave it half my song to hold,
And sent it back to heaven.

Now oft anon, as in a dream,
O'er sculptured heights ascending,
I hear a song — my song, but now,
It has another ending.

With no other models available, this is where Purdy began. Why he didn't heed the advice he must have had in abundance — to find a job with a future, and stick to writing as a hobby — is beyond ordinary comprehension.

After the war Purdy found himself in Vancouver again, where he worked in a mattress factory from 1950 to 1955. Then it was back east to Montreal for two years, to the fertile and combative milieu that included Irving Layton, Louis Dudek, Frank Scott, P. K. Page, and Milton Acorn — Purdy by now having resolved to make himself into a great poet. In 1957 he and his wife built a small house in Ameliasburgh — on Roblin Lake, south of Trenton. And there, with no cash, they settled in: Eurithe to earn their keep, Al to write. Albeit with an acute sense that he had made nothing of his life so far, that perhaps he was a permanent failure.

◆

In 1960, to pause here at Roblin Lake, Purdy was forty-two. He was reading omnivorously, and since 1955 he had published three chapbooks. He'd outgrown *The Enchanted Echo*. But he still hadn't produced more than a handful of poems worth keeping.

Some of the reasons for his slowness must lie in the inscrutable rhythms of any writer's development. But from the vantage of twenty-five years later, it's hard to resist the conclusion that he was trying, however obscurely, to reinvent modern poetry on his own terms. It was a tall order. About 1952 he had been goaded by a friend into reading the classics, particularly the moderns. The effect was drastic. Consciously or not, he'd had to accept that the formal tradition was bankrupt, at least for his own imagination. Rhyme, metrical rhythm, fixed stanza forms, and the stock poetical attitudes that Purdy had been parading — these were drawn from a literary universe in which the rough-hewn autodidact from Trenton could never be more than an outsider. If he wanted to become his own large clumsy aching generous contrary eloquent awestricken self in words, he would have to set aside the whole of traditional poetry, and start back at square one. In his mid-thirties, he would have to recommence his apprenticeship in earnest.

And at that point, an apparently perverse spirit of independence had taken hold. He would not put himself to school with the accepted modern masters: not Yeats or Eliot, not Pound or Williams. Nor would he settle into one of the newer styles, with Auden or Dylan Thomas. For better or worse, he would negotiate an independent passage — from the weird time warp of (say) 1910, where he'd been stuck, to his own here and now. But there was a price to pay for this stubbornness. Already a late developer, he would now have to spend another full decade discovering what Al Purdy sounded like.

Mind you, he did gain some momentum by wrestling with other poets. In the mid-1950s he wrote like Dylan Thomas for a year or two. And around 1958, he tried out Irving Layton's verbal flamboyance and self-assertive stance. But the results were more compacted and stiff-jointed than what he was reaching for, and soon he was pressing ahead again. What he needed was a way of writing that fitted him like a skin; that let him enact his own way of inhabiting the world, speak its native inflections. What his hands could touch, what his nerve-ends knew — these would be the final test of words. Along with his inner ear.

A clear marker in the transition is the lively but exasperating "Gilgamesh and Friend," from 1959:

> Eabani, or Enkidu, made by an itinerant goddess
> From clay, hairy, perhaps human,
> Destined to have carbuncles, goiter, fear of death —
>
> Became friend of beasts, notable in that
> He learned their language (played the flute?),
> Was weaned from animals by a courtesan …
>
> (How?) Joined Gilgamesh to initiate heroism
> (First known ism?) in the Sumerian microcosm.
> Killed bulls, wizards, monsters like Shumbaba
>
> (Who had no genitals, thank goodness!) in a cedar forest …

By now Purdy has started to loosen up. And the play of energy in the speaker's consciousness is the pent-up *something* that had been trying, all along, to find its way into his poetry. Letting that energy invade the process of composition — so that the poet simultaneously sketches his subject (like a musical theme) and embroiders it with fancy honks and playful suppositions (like a series of improvised variations) — this looks like the next step Purdy had to take. … Except it isn't working yet. The set stanza form just gets in the way, a residue of alien convention. And the ostensible subject, Gilgamesh and friend, disappears beneath the avalanche of wisecracks.

By 1960, dug in at Roblin Lake, Purdy was finally in motion. But it still wasn't clear that he was going anywhere of poetic interest.

◆

What happened during the next two years was an abrupt quantum leap, of the sort that defies explanation whenever it occurs. In his collection of 1962, *Poems for All the Annettes*, there are still misfires. But in the best poems, the mature Purdy simply vaults free of three decades of marking time, in a riot of exuberant, full-throated energy.

Now the closed forms of the past are spronged open with a vengeance, releasing a headlong, sometimes dizzying cascade. As in "Archaeology of Snow," where the line breaks, indents and phrasing seem configured by the play of unpredictable energy, rather than being poured into a pre-existing mould:

> Bawdy tale at first
>   what happened
> in the snow
> what happens
>   in bed or anywhere I said
>   oh Anna
>   here —
>   here —
> here —
>   here —
>   here — ...

Once having discovered this degree of freedom, Purdy would settle into a more restrained use of multiple margins and spray-gun layout. But claiming such plasticity in the way a poem lands on the page seems to have been a necessary part of the breakthrough to his own voice.

And the *pace* of a poem is something he can control with virtuosity. Now certain line breaks occur after a word like "and" or "the" (dragging the reader on to the next line, to complete the unit of thought), while others coincide with a natural pause (recreating the breathers the imagination takes, as it finds its way ahead). A canny modulation between these two kinds of line break was another sign of his maturing craft.

The poem has become an act of discovery, rather than a list of things discovered. It's full of particulars. And it is fluid, constantly in process; often the lid is not quite banged shut at the end. Now he can catch a wide range of tonalities, from a headlong clatter to a delicate, murmuring equipoise: "Briefly briefly all things / make the sounds / that are theirs —." Or to the grave, almost liturgical hush of "Remains of an Indian Village":

Standing knee-deep in the joined earth
of their weightless bones,
in the archaeological sunlight,
the trembling voltage of summer,
in the sunken reservoirs of rain,
standing waist-deep in the criss-cross
rivers of shadows,
in the village of nightfall,
the hunters silent and women
bending over dark fires,
I hear their broken consonants ...

At forty-four, Purdy had come into his own — with all sirens going. The long apprenticeship was over. He had found his way to an open poetry which could be brash, adventurous, tender, self-mocking, sublime; within which he could move in any direction with gusto and abandon.

He had made the same journey, from a closed to an open poetic universe, that other major talents accomplished in the twentieth century. But he'd done it in characteristically maverick fashion. He had refused to read Whitman, Pound, or Williams, whose free rhythms and vernacular diction would have made them obvious mentors. (He particularly loathed Whitman.) And he'd made temporary stopovers with Thomas and Layton, who were not pointing in the direction he would finally take. D. H. Lawrence's poetry would become a touchstone for him — but only after 1965, when his own formation was complete.

Purdy had found an independent path, to an unmarked destination, essentially by himself. And in the process, he had become a genuine original.

◆

In *The Cariboo Horses*, three years later, Purdy consolidated everything he had learned in the earlier leap, and carried it further. There is now a wonderful sure-footedness in the rangy, loping gait which had become his signature — with its ability to open out into vast perspectives of space and time, then narrow down to a single moment or image. It was with this volume that he reached a wide critical and popular audience. And the spate of good and great poems began, which have taken on normative status in our literature.

One advance was a new assurance in identifying his subject matter. For years I thought of *Cariboo Horses* as the book in which Purdy claimed his Canadian themes — perhaps because it includes "The Country North of Belleville," one of his first unequivocal masterpieces. But what's startling, on returning to the book, is how *much* of Purdy's home ground it claims. Here are the portraits, the vignettes, the early memories, poems of place, jokey breakneck yarns, on-the-spot reportage, har-de-har asides, delicate evocations of love and the natural world, broad satire, distant times and places: sex and death and poetry, the galaxy and Roblin Lake.

Above all, it's the book with the magisterial authority of lines like these:

> Old fences drift vaguely among the trees
>   a pile of moss-covered stones
> gathered for some ghost purpose
> has lost meaning under the meaningless sky

— they are like cities under water
and the undulating green waves of time
are laid on them ...
("The Country North of Belleville")

With the appearance of *The Cariboo Horses*, in Purdy's forty-seventh year, this story of late-blooming, interminable, and heroic apprenticeship comes to completion. We need a different approach than the chronological to take the measure of the next three decades.

2. The Process

Surveying Purdy's mature poetry as a single body of work, stretching from 1962 to the present, reveals some large recurring features. One is the vision of *process* which informs his poetry. (I'll let the term gather its meaning as we proceed.)

This vision is first of all historical. It's conceivable that growing up in Loyalist country (albeit with no great family stress on tradition) contributed to Purdy's sense of organic continuity in time. Certainly he has written often and well about the persistence of the past in that milieu. "Father and grandfathers are here," he says, "grandmothers and mother / farmers and horsebreakers / tangled in my flesh / who built my strength for a journey" ("In the Dream of Myself"). And in the two poems entitled "Roblin's Mills" he concentrates so hard on the nineteenth-century inhabitants of his village that he is granted contact with their lives, and communes with their "departures and morning rumours / gestures and almost touchings." Though they must subside again into the past, their continuity can now be gravely affirmed: "they had their being once / and left a place to stand on."

Even when the legacy of the past is indecipherable, that very message of obliterated purpose tells Purdy something about his roots.

In "The Country North of Belleville," he meditates on inscrutable stone-piles and fences that no longer enclose anything, their farms long abandoned. And the choric lament rises in him: "This is the country of our defeat." Both the strength and the failures of the past live on in time.

◆

For Purdy, time is a continuum that permits a commerce of dead with living, living with dead — rather than being a wasteland, say, or an executioner. And so his sense of time passing is bittersweet, rather than merely bitter.

On the one hand, he laments what perishes. In "Elegy for a Grandfather," he expands on the old man's death to mourn for everything that dies:

> and earth takes him as it takes more beautiful things:
> populations of whole countries,
> museums and works of art,
> and women with such a glow
> it makes their background vanish
>   they vanish too,
> and Lesbos' singer in her sunny islands
> stopped when the sun went down —

Yet on the other hand, things don't just die. Thus he can remark (in "Temporizing in the Eternal City") on how "the past turned inside out / protrudes slightly into the present." Such continuity in time may not remove the scandal of transience and death, but it qualifies them in a nourishing way. Looking at the sculpture of Beatrice, he observes "something crouching there / joining the cadences of eternity."

◆

So far, Purdy can be seen as having a sense of the partnership of human beings through time — as indeed he does. But to stop there would be to miss everything weird, wonderful, and distinct in his vision of space-time as a process.

We can glimpse this vision as early as "Night Song for a Woman" (perhaps his first fully mature poem, written in 1958). It's a mysterious little piece, truly a night song.

> A few times only, then away,
> leaving absence akin to presence
> in the changed look of
> buildings
>   an inch off centre —
>
> All things enter
> into me so softly I am
> aware of them
>   not myself
> the mind is sensuous
>   as the body
>   I am a sound
> out of hearing past
> Arcturus
>   still moving outward
>
> — if anyone were to listen
> they'd know
>   about humans

Something has happened to Purdy "a few times only, then away" — but what is it? The poem doesn't appear to say, though perhaps "all things enter into me" gestures at an answer. Again, how does Purdy suddenly find himself on this extraordinary jaunt out past Arcturus? And what is it that people would "know about humans" if they listened? Finally, on a very different tack: what enables these disconnected snatches to hang together at all? Palpably they do, in a breathless murmuring which seems suspended in eerie silence. But what is the source of their coherence?

We won't try to answer these questions yet. But it's evident that the universe according to Purdy operates on unfamiliar principles. It's not just that he can suddenly mutate into "a sound / out of hearing past / Arcturus / still moving outward" — but that the phenomenon is taken so casually for granted. Slipping across the galaxy is as much a matter of course as slipping across the street.

And once we recognize that, we can see that the same thing keeps happening — with all sorts of variations — throughout Purdy's work. Take a step in any direction and you find yourself in the nineteenth century, in long-ago Samarkand, in the Upper Cretaceous or outer space. The cosmos of Purdy's poetry is one in which familiar laws of movement in both space and time can be suspended without warning, and a different set of principles can take over. A second or alternate universe is latent in the familiar one, and it can assert itself at any time. What's intriguing is to chart the behaviour of this parallel reality — the cosmos of *process*.

◆

In "Hockey Players," a game is suddenly detonated when three players swerve out of quotidian space, and into the alternate cosmos. They end up "skating thru the smoky end boards out / of sight and climbing up the appalachian highlands / and racing breast to breast across laurentian barrens." In itself the moment is fanciful, even a bit forced. But the underlying experience — of swerving out of the conventional world, and then covering ground so quickly that space collapses into a blur of simultaneity — is pure Purdy.

In "The Cariboo Horses," he watches cowboys riding into 100 Mile House on their "half-tame bronco rebels." He resists the impulse to romanticize the horses; yet even as he does he finds himself carried elsewhere and elsewhen, transfigured in contemplation of "the ghosts of horses battering thru the wind / whose names were the winds' common usage / whose life was the sun's." Only at the end of the poem does he return to the scene before him. It's a remarkable affirmation of parallel universes — of a day-to-day world, and a larger, more luminous one. And in the alternate universe, points far separated in space and time are simultaneous.

Again, standing "At the Athenian Market," Purdy moves into a kind of lucid trance. Now a pile of oranges is "involved with converging lines / of light Phidias the sculptor / laboured over half an hour / ago." And as the sight of the living girls in the marketplace carries him deeper into trance, he moves to union with "long ago girls" — and then, unexpectedly, further back still, to the first emergence of life from primordial waters, and to the very beginnings of evolution, "before these Greek cities / before the sea was named / before us all." Yet in truth, Purdy doesn't even seem to be "moving back"; this is a stillness which goes beyond the wild canter of "The Hockey Players," and participates in other points in space-time without stirring an inch.

The poem is characteristic in that it sounds the note of lived, authentic exaltation precisely as it enters the aspect which seems the most remote from "real life" — that is, the intuition that all time and space are simultaneous. It's at this juncture that Purdy's poetry regularly takes on the nostril-flare or hush, and the quirky, kindled gait and diction, which make it irreplaceable — and which feel utterly unforced, at home in a mystery they know first-hand, "as the days and nights join hands / when everything becomes one thing" ("The Dead Poet"). The intuition feels more real than mundane reality.

The distant past juts into the immediate present; far away is near at hand. Space-time is plastic, elastic, fantastic. We don't yet know what that signifies. But there are examples by the hundred in Purdy's work; start reading with this in mind and it crops up everywhere, this "simultaneity of things / ... the instant of the dinosaurs / whose instant I am part of" ("Lost in the Badlands"). The cosmos of process is close to being the primary universe of his poetry.

◆

I have been speaking of Purdy's parallel cosmos, and referring to it as one of process. So far, the meaning of "process" seems to be mainly that a great deal of high-speed traffic goes on in the space-time continuum.

But there's more to it than that. For it is also characteristic of the process that it is chock-a-block with things which are incommensurable with one another, yet nonetheless coexist. Sometimes in discord, at other times flowing into one another. Time and again the poem presents, not a single reality which would enforce a single-keyed response, but that reality and its opposite — or (more subtly) two or three further realities which chime off the first, in a discordant but richly complex music of being. That's how the world *is*. Nothing comes single; everything skids into the larger process, and by the very act of existing implicates its incommensurable brothers and lovers and foes and a bad joke and grandparents and death and the dinosaurs, not to mention intergalactic space and a hangover and spring and the first evolving rampant protozoa.

So the world provokes incompatible responses — as a matter of daily course. Celebration and elegy simultaneously; or a fusion of raucous laughter, grief, and awe of an almost unbearable delicacy. Much of the energy of Purdy's work goes into delivering this Heraclitean flux intact. Our categorizing minds might prefer to keep segments of the world in airtight compartments. But the segments don't cooperate.

◆

There are also poems in which the sense of simultaneity goes beyond the normal processes of time altogether. These are poems of ecstasy; they intuit an eternal *now*, in which every moment of past, present, and future participates, in some unfathomable way surviving its own disappearance.

Often Purdy moves into this ecstatic dimension as he contemplates the physical world, and finds himself held in a mysterious under-silence:

in a pile of old snow
under a high wall
a patch of brilliant
yellow dog piss
glows, and joins
things in the mind.
Sometimes I stand still,
like a core at the centre
of my senses, hidden and still —
All the heavy people,
clouds and tangible buildings,
enter and pass thru me:
stand like a spell
of the wild gold sunlight,
knowing the ache stones have,
how mountains suffer,
and a wet blackbird feels
flying past in the rain.
This is the still centre,
an involvement in silences —

("Winter Walking")

What is the meaning of this "rare arrival / of something entirely beyond us" ("Time Past/Time Now")? Sometimes Purdy parses it explicitly as the moment in which things reveal their eternal nature:

This incident:
                    sitting with friends
in the chalet restaurant on top of Mount Royal
talking of a tree swaying back and forth in the wind,
leaving no silvery whip marks of its travelling self
                    or proof of passage.
                                        But we say
"That tree will always be there,
flogging the air forever." ...

("Method for Calling Up Ghosts")

The intuition cannot be translated into conventional thought, of course. And Purdy is so suspicious of mystification of any kind that he mostly backs away from pronouncements on the subject, sometimes from doing anything more than pointing to it cryptically. Often he contents himself with evoking the feel of the eternal moment through the hush and susurration of the words themselves:

They are so different these small ones
their green hair shines
they lift their bodies high in light
they droop in rain and move in unison
toward some lost remembered place
we came from like a question
like a question and the answer
nobody remembers now
no one can remember ...

("The Nurselog")

Mind you, to concentrate exclusively on these glimpses of an eternal *now* is to create a one-sided version of the poetry. Purdy is just as concerned with the horror and the boredom of the world as with its murmurs of glory. But those murmurs are worth identifying; they will help us to fathom what makes the process cohere.

3. Polyphony

We move now to one of the most dazzling aspects of Purdy's writing: his command of *polyphony*, his ability to orchestrate many different voices. Few readers will traverse twenty lines without becoming aware of the constant shifts in diction and pacing and tone, the squawks and blips as Purdy's consciousness intrudes and recedes, the startling turnarounds from redneck coarseness to a supple middle style to soaring passages of joy and lamentation. Purdy is one of the living masters of voice.

And at this point, we can discern why "finding his voice" was so difficult, and so crucial. The voice of his poems would have to mime the nature of his subject matter — the process of what-is, and himself in it. But the nature of the process is to be protean, chameleonic, constantly swerving and bucking and passing into its own opposite in the blink of an eye. Only when the voice of his poetry became as manifold and self-renewing as the process itself would Purdy be able to write the poems that beckoned him. He needed a polyvocal medium, one that could embody his sense of what the world is like.

It would be easy to present five quotations, or fifty, that speak in different voices. And that would indicate Purdy's astonishing tonal range. But it wouldn't demonstrate the most important aspect of the matter — which is not simply that he uses different voices, often in the same poem, but that he's capable of shifting from one to the next in a seamless way, one that mimes a cosmos in which all things flow.

This is not the hard-edge mosaic technique of a Pound, say, where fragment A comes in one voice, fragment B in another, and the two are banged down consecutively with no transition. This jump-cut technique — juxtaposing voices in a discontinuous mosaic — issues properly from Pound's vision of things. It has been the main polyphonic tradition in this century; it has even been followed by poets who don't share Pound's vision, but who lack the resources to find their own way of writing polyphonically.

Purdy's technique, which lets him modulate seamlessly through a great range of voices, issues from *his* own vision of the process — his audition of the process, we might say. The craft of a poetry like this — a craft of morphing or segueing the voice — has not been extensively explored. Yet it is crucial to hearing his work on its own wavelength, and hence to understanding it at all.

To see how his polyphony works, we should examine the vocal trajectory of one poem from start to finish. To keep things manageable, we'll take a short piece.

Love at Roblin Lake

My ambition as I remember and
I always remember was always
to make love vulgarly and immensely
        as the vulgar elephant doth
                & immense reptiles did
        in the open air openly
        sweating and grunting together
        and going
                "BOING   BOING   BOING"
                                                making
every lunge a hole in the great dark
for summer cottagers to fall into at a later date
and hear inside faintly (like in a football
stadium when the home team loses)
ourselves still softly
        going
                "boing   boing   boing"

as the vulgar elephant doth
    & immense reptiles did
in the star-filled places of earth
that I remember we left behind long ago
and forgotten everything after
on our journey into the dark

Consider the poem's broad movement in space-time. Purdy starts by conflating his own lovemaking with that of elephants and "immense reptiles," the latter presumably being the dinosaurs. There is already a fusion of times, though merely because the contemporary lover is wishing himself back to a more primitive past. But starting about line eleven, and then much more rapidly in the last four lines, there's an effect like an infinite camera pullback in a movie. Suddenly we see all the traffic of earth — the ambitious lover, the elephants, the long-ago dinosaurs, the planet itself — diminishing to the size of specks, as we unexpectedly pull away from them. This reverse zoom is taking place in time; we are moving into the evolutionary present, away from the "star-filled places of earth" (apparently a time-layer when humans still coupled with the unself-conscious instinct of beasts). And the pullback is also taking place in space; we are receding from the little planet earth into the intergalactic dark, where human and pre-human concerns are so far away they seem both infinitely small and infinitely poignant. The sense of bittersweet awe at the end is unnerving, especially since we have swerved such a great distance in so few lines.

What gives me goosebumps in this poem is the way the process of tonal change enacts the process being described. This is the larger truth about Purdy's poetry that we're after. He does not simply write *about* the process; he keeps miming it in the movement of the poem's voice, its vocal trajectory. Let's retrace "Love at Roblin Lake" with that in mind. For it's clear that the poem starts in one voice, and ends in another. But Purdy's skill at modulating voices is so great that it's far less clear how we got from one to the other.

The piece begins with the speaker as a bit of a bumbler, who gets himself tangled in words at the very outset: "My ambition as I remember and / I always remember was always ..." After this abrupt little nosedive, the *grosseries* the speaker is about to deliver about making love "vulgarly and immensely" may give us a yuck or two, may even speak for the sweatily horny strain in us. But given the clumsy, almost coarse tone of his speaking voice, they seem unlikely to rise much above that level. (Few readers will be thinking any of this consciously as they proceed, of course. If the voice works, it will simply exert a tactful, preconscious pressure on our reading, setting the terms in which we experience the poem as a whole.)

The first surprise comes with the archaic "doth," which pops out at the mention of bygone pachyderms and dinosaurs. With that little tonal blip as the giveaway, the speaker now appears as a more sophisticated man: as one who enjoys playing roles, including that of a clodhopper — rather than simply *being* a clodhopper.

The description of rutting, complete with comic-book "BOING BOING BOING," picks up the note of har-de-har comedy again — only to dissolve into the weird, serpentine, but surprisingly persuasive image of the phallic trench as a hole in the dark which traps summer cottagers who turn out to be ourselves as well, now inside a football stadium and raising only muted cheers because the home team is losing. Wherever the poem is going, it's clearly nowhere we could have predicted at the start (a mere dozen lines ago). But the changing tone of the piece is itself guiding us through this free, uncharted trajectory in poetic space. By now the voice has become plain, yet sinewy and evocative. We've shifted away from the broad, slapdash tonality of the opening, and though it's not at all clear where we're headed, the voice now feels like a trustworthy guide.

Next we discover that we are both inside the stadium, making love and going "*boing*," and outside it, somewhere in undifferentiated space. And our increasing distance from the stadium action, our accelerating pullback, is mimed as the original "BOING BOING BOING" fades to "*boing boing boing*." Now the vulgar elephant and the immense reptiles bear a kind of pathos of distance about them, as they echo their earlier appearance. And with the stammer of broken phrases which concludes the poem, we move into an eerie, hedgerow sublime. It may take a few readings before we can analyze where we are, physically or psychically — but at an emotional and imaginative level, the heart-wrenched, awestruck tone of the ending has already told us:

going
"*boing boing boing*"
as the vulgar elephant doth
& immense reptiles did
in the star-filled places of earth
that I remember we left behind long ago
and forgotten everything after
on our journey into the dark

We are watching the funny, sexy, absurd, and poignant dance of mating, performed by one couple, by human beings, by all species that have dwelt on earth. We view them both from within the experience and from a remove that is some place like death, or eternity — where laughter, choked-back tears, and a cosmic hush commingle.

The changing trajectory of voice, together with the sweep of shifting perspectives, has helped Purdy to limn a process in which near and far, past and present, comic and tragic are somehow simultaneous.

4. *Tremendum*

WE HAVE A POETRY CHARACTERIZED BY ZOOM PERSPECTIVES ON space-time; by the simultaneity of things that may or may not jibe; by moments of luminous stillness; and by constant vocal shifts, which guide us through the process according to Purdy. What do they signify?

Purdy gives us a day-to-day world that is unmistakably the cranky, suffering, shades-of-grey place we inhabit. But at the same time he gives us an experience that keeps breaking through in moments of epiphany. This is an encounter with what theologians call *mysterium tremendum* — holy otherness. An appropriate response to the *tremendum* is awe, joy, terror, gratitude. We've seen a number of these ecstatic moments, where time seems to lock for the speaker, and the physical world is both utterly present and wholly transparent, a window into some ineffable dimension where he is at once lost and at home. There are many, many more.

For Purdy, such experience of *tremendum* is always mediated through things of the world. "My Grandfather's Country" ponders the way it impinges through place, and occurs with its own particularity in each locale. In the desert, for example, where "a man can walk and walk into identical distance / like an arrow lost in its own target." Or in the high Arctic, where:

> ... there are seas in the north so blue
> that a polar bear can climb his own wish and walk the sky
> and wave on wave of that high blue washes over the mind
> and sings to each component part of the hearing blood
> a radiance that burns down the dark buildings of night
> and sings for 24 hours a day of long sea-days ...

Frequently, as he says in "The Darkness," such experience conveys "some lost kind of coherence / I've never found in people / or in myself for that matter." Thus in "The Beavers of Renfrew" he senses that the beavers still know

> the secret of staying completely still,
> allowing ourselves to catch up
> with the shadow just ahead of us
> we have lost,
> when the young world was a cloudy room
> drifting thru morning stillness — ...

And sensing this holy otherness in the daily world, he enters an eternal *now*. Everything that has ever meant itself, ever been at all, seems still to live undiminished in this dimension. Hence everything is simultaneous with everything else — "as if all we are / co-exists in so many forms / we encounter the entire race / of men just by being / alive here" ("Archaeology of Snow").

This eternal *now* is not situated by Purdy anywhere specifiable: not in a heaven, nor an afterlife, nor art (though it can mediate the intuition), nor his own mind (though it loves to embroider the moment). He has no theories about it; all he can do is recreate its onset on the page, magnificently, as direct experience. Most of the time he scarcely seems to know what to make of its incursions. And the religions which offer a framework for the experience just make him snort atheistically. It's a pure, intuited condition which keeps barging into the flux of the quotidian, without altering the mundane terms in which he lives the rest of his life.

Purdy recreates the daily world as it appears in and out of the light of *tremendum*. His life work, in all its variety, stands as a series of responses to that central intuition.

And this makes sense of the distinctive elements of process we have observed in his work. It explains the constant zoom perspectives: to whirl from Roblin Lake to the early life of stone two hundred million years ago — that is simply to mime the eternal *now*, in which all time and space are a dance of simultaneity. What's more, in that transcendent moment the heterogeneous things of the world coexist in a kind of charged coherence — without being forced into an abstract unity. So that is how he records them. And to let the poem's voice ripple through a spectrum of changes — that too is to mime the luminous flow in the *tremendum*, which daily things bespeak in their moments of glory.

That is, the jumps and segues in his poems, their insistence on overlaid or clashing realities, their polyphony — these take their deepest origin from the intuition of *mysterium tremendum* in the day-to-day world. Purdy's unique way of moving in a poem, and of orchestrating its elements, derives from his fundamental vision of what the world is like. Which is to say, his artistry is mature.

◆

Providing the term is kept free of associations with dogma and churchy attitudes, this vision is properly called religious — though not theistic. But Purdy still doesn't pretend to know what it *means*, that such incandescence lurks in the quotidian. The experience is indelible; its significance is opaque. Questions about God or immortality receive no answer from within the process. The tentative prayer in "The Darkness" is about as close as he's let himself come to addressing the "spirit of everyplace / guardian beyond the edge of chaos" as though something could hear him. And it would be the cheapest effrontery on a reader's part to march in and explain this impulse in his poetry. Or baptize it. Or even label it possessively. My terms for it, "*tremendum*" and "the eternal *now*," are meant to honour the mystery, not straitjacket it. And the ecstatic power and incandescent grace which the poetry takes on as it enters the kinetic stillness furnish all the validation that I, for one, could ask.

◆

But Purdy frets at times that he may be simply projecting the movements of his own mind onto the world: "I mistrust the mind-quality that tempts me / to embroider and exaggerate things" ("The Horseman of Agawa"). And it's true; sometimes he himself is clearly inventing the wild leaps which a poem enacts. The result can be a willed, rather frantic exercise.

But the tall tales and goofy exaggerations don't pretend to be anything other than that. And far from calling in question his deeper treatment of the process, they seem like a coltish retracing of what his intuition already knows. For Purdy writes from a profoundly intuitive imagination, which can tap into some ache and transcendence at the heart of things, and kindle in response. The ecstatic passages of "My Grandfather's Country," "The Beavers of Renfrew," "Night Song for a Woman" — these unmistakably touch grace, whatever its name may be. As do dozens of others. Entering these moments in the poetry, we sense a great hush which sustains the disparate things that are, and renders their all-over-the-map simultaneity and their vocal flow coherent. Such moments don't seem willed by the poet; they seem sponsored by being.

◆

But to end on that lofty note would convey a false impression — not of the vision which animates Purdy's poetry, but of the poems themselves. For one thing, they often report on a daily world which shows no trace of *tremendum*, and which can be unrelievedly brutal at times. Some of these more humdrum pieces are vigorous and engaging; others are just prosy. But that merely shows that Purdy spends much of his time in a middle state, like the rest of us. He doesn't have nonstop entry to the cosmos of process.

Of greater interest is the compulsion he feels, to avoid giving even a sublime poem too much polish, too final and finished a surface. There is an offhandedness, even a slapdash quality, which is clearly an intrinsic part of the way he wants a poem to *be*. That this is a deliberate policy is evident if we examine his revisions. They can go on for years, decades even, and frequently they polish individual passages to a burnished glow. But often the piece as a whole is left with an in-process, written-while-experienced feel to it; sometimes revision takes it further in that direction. This is an imagination which refuses to be housebroken. And if we approach even a classic Purdy poem too reverently, expecting a rarified masterpiece, it's likely to light a cigar, tell a corny joke, get up and leave halfway through the conversation. The high style comes and goes as it pleases — as at the end of "Spring Song":

> someone breathed or sighed or spoke
> and everything rearranged itself
> from is to was the white moon tracks
> her silver self across the purple night
> replacing time with a celestial
> hour glass halfway between a girl
> and woman I forgot till she comes jiggling
> back from the dark mailbox at last migawd
> hosanna in the lowest mons veneris
> I will never get to change the goddam oil

Purdy is a plain man visited by towering intuitions, not a beatified mystic. And his loose-jointed, bantering middle style affords a complex artistic leverage. It lets him acknowledge the long dry stretches between epiphanies — by the very act of including that middle voice. It gives him a way of honouring his plebeian origins, as his highfalutin early verse did not. And it provides a kind of ground bass, against which the moments of *tremendum* can register more tellingly when they come along. If he does connect with one of those incandescent moments, it will enter a poem whose voice can then modulate or erupt — thanks to his immense improvisational talents — into the high style of the epiphany, and thereby reenact the process it records.

This vocal strategy accounts for much of the unique temper and form of Purdy's work. The trick for a reader is to settle onto a wavelength that can accommodate, as they occur, both the consciously rough-hewn textures and the inflections of the incandescent. Purdy has in effect redefined "a poem" to mean a piece of writing that plays in the space between those boundaries — never in the same way twice. Across the body of his work, that changing vocal play is what we're invited to enjoy.

5. Native Speaking

THERE ARE OTHER CRITICAL APPROACHES THAT ILLUMINATE Purdy's work. I'll take one more here, considering his poetry as a venture in native speaking.

For half a century, Purdy has been lugging a preoccupation with the spirit of place back and forth across his homeland. The result has been a series of poems about locales and events which assemble into an imaginative map of Canada — not an exhaustive one, but far more complete than any other writer's. Without itemizing individual poems, we can say he has followed the path of first-hand exploration described in "Transient":

> after a while the eyes digest a country and
> the belly perceives a mapmaker's vision
> in dust and dirt on the face and hands here
> ...

> and the shape of home is under your fingernails
> the borders of yourself grown into certainty

These poems of Canadian place and history are a grand gift to the rest of us.

Purdy has "placed" us in subtler ways as well. For one thing, the imaginative journeys he has taken elsewhere in space-time coalesce into a larger map: this time, an experiential record of what one man has discovered on the planet, and indeed in the universe. (I have in mind his journeys to other times and species, along with the literal globetrotting.) It makes no pretence to being a scholarly world history; the mapmaker's vision is still perceived in the belly and under the fingernails. But the vistas of geological time and interstellar space within which Purdy ranges are breathtaking. And because everything he encounters can be charged with *tremendum*, can reveal itself as part of the luminous process, his record of journeys in the universe stands as a wider poetic cosmology, an ampler account of meaningful order.

What's notable is that Purdy focuses the cosmos from the vantage point of his own home. Sometimes this is explicit; in "News Report at Ameliasburg" he transmits a cacophony of war reports from global history, then winds down with a report on sunset in his own small village. But with or without the explicit reference point, a Canada-centred relationship of "there" to "here," of "then" to "now," is defined right in the idiom and perspective of the speaker, who is unmistakably a contemporary Canuck by the name of Al Purdy.

And now there is a new thing on earth: a poetic cosmology focused concentrically around Roblin Lake, southeastern Ontario, Canada, North America, planet earth, all space-time. It does not invalidate visions of order centred elsewhere. But here is a body of major poetry — a muscular, roomy, and persuasive vision of coherence — centred in our own here and now. Such a thing did not exist before.

◆

To write as a native speaker is not just a matter of exploring Canadian places and deeds, however. Nor even of mapping the world with Canada as the imaginative centre. At a deeper level, it is to embody in words our historic modes of dwelling here — not by describing them at arm's length, but by *enacting* them on the page. And Purdy has articulated our native reflexes and tensions right in the musculature and movement of his poems. That too has opened imaginative room for us to dwell in.

It would take a whole further essay to explore Purdy's work from this perspective. But let me identify at least some of the native reflexes which inform his work. No one of them is uniquely Canadian, but taken together they have much to do with who we've been here.

The first concerns the *tremendum*. Throughout history, different things have served as the vehicle for encounter with holy otherness: sexual love, battle, contemplation, for example. It is central to our history and imagination in this part of the world that we approach the *tremendum* by knowing the vast, extreme and eerie land we inhabit. The mystique is strong, even among confirmed city dwellers. And Purdy's poems of the land embody that reflex to a singular degree.

A second native reflex is that of instinctively locating our fragile human settlements, even the big cities, in a surrounding space of almost inconceivable magnitude, and as tenuous moments in a field of time which loops back at once to Stone Age humans and out through intergalactic light years. For that is the nature of our dwelling here. The land is vast. Much of the ground our feet or tires traverse was formed eons ago. And the period of colonial settlement is such a thin patina, often less than two hundred years in depth, that once we penetrate even a hair's breadth beyond it, we are swept into millennia of Indigenous dwelling (which remains a mystery to most Canadians), and then into vast reaches of pre-human time. In Purdy, that sense of johnny-come-lately dwelling contributes to the reflex of temporal and spatial hopscotching that we've observed.

In "The Runners," a speaker declares, "I think the land knows we are here, / I think the land knows we are strangers." That double declaration reveals a third reflex — a deep and positive ambivalence in the Canadian makeup, which resonates across many aspects of our lives. "The land knows we are here." It antedates us, exerts a claim upon us, and gives us a home if we come to it knowing our place. Hence we are not free to simply master and remake it according to the dictates of our own wills, as has been a dominant American pattern; rather we are free to *belong* to it, even if gingerly. But at the same time, "the land knows we are strangers." We do not have a history of countless generations in a secure dwelling place, where we domesticated nature, and felt safe (till recently, at least) in its interpenetration with civilization. In this regard, we are not like European human beings.

So each declaration is both true and false to who we are. We exist in their continuing tension, in which we are compelled by both the Old World and the American version of the New — yet neither one by itself feels like us. It is a destiny of incomplete or multiple answers, of ironic perspectives, of perpetual lack of full definition. Purdy's poetry, with its grand articulation of being both strange and at home in this place — a sensitive brawler in taverns, a learnèd rube — embodies that tension in its very fabric.

A fourth reflex has to do with eloquence, delicacy of feeling, amplitude of spirit. It is central to our original social and cultural heritage that these things can be expressed, but only if they are cloaked in defensive irony. And once they have been revealed, we hear them echoing in a still vaster silence, and subsiding into it very quickly again. Purdy's poems enact that stutter-step reflex, time and again, in their emotional trajectory.

In its embodiment of these deep, historic modes of being here, his poetry articulates who we are — *places* us in our home space — to an unprecedented degree. In speaking of this, of course, we can't homogenize all Canadians into a single mould. People with other modes of dwelling engrained in their marrow are no less Canadian for that. But whether or not we like every reflex the poems embody, they *are* many of us. And so we can move through this poetry without having to turn ourselves into denizens of somewhere else, merely to follow its natural lines of movement. At this profound, almost preconscious level, Purdy is a supremely accomplished native speaker.

6. Purdy's Stature

How are we to assess Al Purdy? It seems to me incontrovertible that he is one of the substantial poets in English of the twentieth century. Of the hundreds of poems he has published, some fifteen or twenty place him in the rank of poets like W. H. Auden, D. H. Lawrence, Robert Frost, Dylan Thomas. If we have to realign our notion of what great poetry looks like to accommodate his best work — and it's part of his achievement that we do — that is scarcely a novel experience, when a writer of stature comes along.

There's something more as well. If we step back several paces, we can find a broader perspective in which to situate Purdy, one that sheds fuller light on his achievement.

From the sixteenth century on, the imperial nations of Europe spread their languages and cultural paradigms around the planet:

English, French, Spanish, Portuguese, and to a lesser extent Dutch. For both better and worse. And during the twentieth century, after a long colonial period, literature in those languages became polycentric, as the former colonies found their voices — rivalling and sometimes surpassing the imperial centres. The most impressive contemporary example is that of Spanish and Portuguese writing in Latin America, but the process has been repeated around the globe, in recent decades with gathering potency.

This has not just been a matter of poets and novelists in the ex-colonies learning to write well in the fashion of their erstwhile mentors. The language of the metropolitan imagination has had to be unlearned in the provinces, even as it was being learned from. A long hard struggle of independence has been necessary, for writers of the hinterlands to imagine their own time and place, to become articulate as native speakers. The titans have been those who first broke through to indigenous articulacy, who subverted and recast the forms of the metropolitan imagination so as to utter the truths of the hinterland. Generally they've done so with a rare fusion of high artistry and folk, even populist, imagination. It's clear that Whitman, Melville, Neruda, García Márquez are among the founders who claimed a nation's patrimony this way — and in the process recast the imaginative vocabulary of their medium. Without pretending to exhaustive knowledge of the subject, I suspect their number also includes Dario, Amado, Guillén, Asturias, Césaire, Miron, Senghor, Walcott.

In the case of countries colonized by England, the situation is complicated one stage further. American writers made their breakthrough to native speaking very early, in the nineteenth century. In the result, American literature went on to such strengths that by the mid-twentieth century, anglophone writers elsewhere had to free themselves from the hegemony of both Britain and the United

States. Such a situation does not exist in French, Spanish, or Portuguese. But that anomaly recognized, the challenge of speaking native among English-speaking writers in Africa, India, Canada, Australia, the Caribbean, and elsewhere has been parallel to that faced by a Neruda or a Senghor.

And that situates Al Purdy in a wider context. He has been one of the giants of the recurrent process in which, language by language and country by country over the last seventy years, the hinterlands of empire have broken through to universal resonance by learning to speak local. Purdy has claimed, and in many ways created, an indigenous imaginative patrimony for English Canada.

To say that is not to denigrate English Canadian poets whose excellence is of other kinds — Irving Layton and Margaret Avison, for a start. Emily Dickinson wasn't called to be Whitman, nor Vallejo Neruda. But in his rootedness, his breadth, and his impulse to forge a native idiom for the imagination, Purdy is one of a distinct breed: the heroic founders, who give their people a voice as they go about their own necessities.

Of course, not all titans are equal in stature. And seen in that lofty company, Purdy may be one of the lesser colossi. But it is among their number that he must be counted.

◆

It is a matter of fact that readers abroad have scarcely begun to discover Al Purdy. Or more accurately, have not yet taken the crucial first step — of hearing this hinterland idiom on its own wavelength, as an instrument capable of genius, at once familiar and foreign. But such tone-deafness in the metropolis is an old story. It is the tough luck of London and New York, which time will rectify.

Meanwhile, for those who can read Purdy on his own wavelength, his poetry is a windfall and a blessing.

Memories of Miron

This is a memorial essay, written for a special "Gaston Miron" issue of the journal Liberté. *It came out in 1997, the year after Miron died.*

I debated what to say about this titan. I couldn't pretend to be an expert on Miron's poetry — least of all when I was addressing Quebecois readers, for whom his work had furnished a kind of daily bread of the heart. Nor could I discuss his wider impact on Quebec society, since I hadn't been there to observe it.

What I did have was a string of personal memories — of a peerless poet, and a noble human being. So I went with that.

MIRON. MIRONS. THE MEMORIES NOW A JUMBLE: THE MAN more luminous than ever.

◆

I remember one late-night session, at a party in Montreal. Was it in the 1970s? There was a piano in the living room, and on the spur of the moment we started improvising. I want to recall it as a triumph, the music transcending languages, boundaries, isms. But in fact, it was a farce.

Gaston played mouth harp, in a rough-hewn rural style he carried off well. For my part, I attacked the piano in an idiom composed equally of boogie, blues, and armageddon, somewhat tempered by my inability to play in any key but C major. Along with a tendency to stretch, shrink, or dispense entirely with the twelve-bar blues form in which we were improvising. It took us about five minutes to clear the room, and another five to realize we couldn't stand the racket ourselves. So we slunk back to the scotch, sheepish comrades in cacophony.

◆

For the Gaston Miron of public record, I have to turn to reference books. Born in 1928, sixty miles north of Montreal — a country boy. Came to Montreal at nineteen, and did pickup jobs while he started to write. Co-founded l'Hexagone, a press which under his direction became the leading poetry publisher in Quebec. A socialist, and passionately for Quebec independence from the start.

And then the poetry. Miron published exactly one full-length collection, *L'homme rapaillé*, in 1970. Yet on its strength he came to be recognized as the godfather of postwar Quebec poetry, and received awards and honours throughout the French-speaking world.

And now the final entry. December 14, 1996: dead of cancer.

◆

My first Miron appeared when I needed him most.

I was thirty-one. Two years previously I'd published *Civil Elegies* — meditations on the checkmate called English Canada. My dear detested homeland: perpetual colony, which had never found the courage to exist as a resonant public space. But then I'd hit a dry spell. And I was paralyzed still; I was no longer satisfied with the *Elegies,* but everything else I tried rang false.

It was in this state that I opened *Ellipse* magazine, in the fall of 1970, at my home in Toronto. I could scarcely believe what I found. It featured translations from a poet called Gaston Miron. And I found myself reading lines like these:

> je n'ai jamais voyagé
> vers autre pays que toi mon pays

and these:

> je te salue, silence
>
> je ne suis plus revenu pour revenir
> je suis arrivé a ce qui commence

There was also an essay by Georges-André Vachon, who spoke of Miron's search for the poetry of his native space. "The poetry of his native space" — that's what *I* was after!

Who *was* this man? And what was he doing inside my nervous system? In English Canada, with the mammoth exception of Al Purdy, nobody wrote on public themes. Or if they did, it was with the greeting-card quaintness of the Maple Leaf school, or else a stentorian patriotism that made me cringe. But to accept that words themselves are cankered with our colonial non-belonging; to recreate that dispossession right in the poem's voice; to wait on political resistance and the word, in silence, to envoice our communal being — this was a kind of artistic heroism I had given up hope of discovering in anyone with the same passport as me. But Miron was palpably the real thing.

For months I fed on that poetry and essay. There was a catalyzing affinity, as if with an older brother I hadn't known was there. Eleven years my senior; a confirming presence in Montreal. And while I don't suggest a direct cause and effect, two years later the dry spell had ended. A revised version of *Civil Elegies* came out, which was much more at home in its skin. And anyone who reads the Miron issue of *Ellipse* will know how profoundly I imbibed him. He helped me to claim more deeply the words of my native space.

◆

Another Miron. A snippet.

I'm sitting at an outdoor table, in a tiny square in Paris. One evening in the '80s. And a woman I've just met is explaining to me that *quality doesn't count*. She is in charge of implementing gender policy at some Canadian cultural agency, I forget which one. She wants none of my chauvinist bullshit about good writing being better than bad writing; she wants fifty-fifty gender parity in grants, with no reference to quality till that is achieved.

I am a fellow-travelling feminist, three thousand miles from home, and I'm thoroughly depressed. Why do good principles always get screwed up? ... At which point, my eye lights on a poster across the square. Holy shit — it's Miron! Big square mug gazing out at us. He was honoured in Paris last week; it's an ad for a reading he gave.

In three leaps I'm across the square, prying the poster off the bricks. I lug it back to the table with an exaggerated sense of relief. The conversation has taken another turn, but the icon will accompany me back to T.O.

Quality counts.

◆

Around 1972, at some event in Montreal, Miron came bounding up to the translator Sheila Fischman. He began quoting from an anthology that included four lines (four lines?) from *Civil Elegies*. Had Sheila ever heard of a guy called Lee? What about commissioning a translation for l'Hexagone? Sheila was complimentary about the poem, and told Gaston of a partial version in French done by Marc Lebel at the University of Sherbrooke. And so that chapter of things began.

But what a large and perfect gesture! Miron gets a buzz of recognition, reading four lines in a language he says he doesn't understand — and out he marches, to usher the whole thing into French.

Once there were men like this. Right in our own time and place.

◆

There's also the poignancy of Miron's own writing project. It shushes me.

A poet intuits a crucial space of words, which has never been filled. It's reserved for the national epic of his homeland — one which will tell its unspoken truths, and thereby help to itch the homeland into existence.

The poet can block in some chunks of the national epic. But unless he pretends that the colonized words which are his vocation are something more genuine, that's all he can do. Block in chunks. It is his failure, and also his triumph, that he will do no more.

Moses Miron. The leader of his people — permitted to glimpse the promised land, but not to enter it.

◆

I remember the first time I met Miron in person, in the spring of 1977. I had come to Montreal to give a reading; Sheila Fischman picked me up after, and we drove to the Carré St. Louis.

I was nervous as all get out. Marc Lebel's translation was moving ahead, but Gaston and I still hadn't met. Now he would learn the truth: I really was a WASP, my French was spotty, I couldn't pass an exam on the semiotics of Quebec poetry. All the liberal guilt in Toronto was churning through my system; I was Bay Street in blue jeans, the Plains of Abraham were about to land on my head. Should I address him as "vous"?

What's odd is how little I remember of the meeting itself. Though perhaps it's not so odd. Because my main recollection is of the man's surpassing warmth, his sheer generosity of spirit. Along with that animal gusto! He took pains to greet me with "tu"; I began to ease. Then, still in the first minute or so, he sprang to his feet and declaimed some lines from the *Elegies*. In English first:

> Many were born in Canada, and living unlived lives they died
> of course but died truncated, stunted, never at
> home in native space and not yet
> citizens of a human body of kind. ...

Then in Marc's French:

> Plusieurs sont nés au Canada, et au terme de vies invécues moururent
> bien sûr mais moururent tronqués, rabougris, jamais chez
> eux dans l'espace natal et toujours pas
> citoyens d'un corps d'espèce humaine. ...

I grinned, and relaxed some more. ... And that was that. We must have gabbed for hours. What did we talk about? Who knows? I hope I conveyed a fraction of what it had meant to read his stuff in *Ellipse*. And like hundreds of others who encountered Gaston, I came away knowing I was special. I'd been met, understood.

◆

There's one thing I never said out loud. Gaston had started the "Collection en tous lieux," to open the door to poetry from outside Quebec. And though much was opaque to me, I could see what a radical step it was, to choose as an early title a book from Toronto. Openness to the world was one thing — but openness to English

Canada? It must have been playing with fire, even for someone as unassailable as Miron.

I wanted to tell him how much I honoured his courage. But doing so would have cheapened it somehow — crossed a line improperly. I was still a member of the erstwhile dominant culture, even if Gaston never treated me as such. And he wasn't breaking the taboo in order to win my approval.

The only way I could find to salute that immense integrity was to take it at face value, and shut up. ... Heigh-ho: the subterranean communication of males. Did Gaston ever know how much I admired him?

◆

In 1979, Miron and Lebel and I drove to a house somewhere north of Montreal. Was it out in the country? We were going to spend the weekend doing a final polish on the translation. And what a marathon it was. We barely slept.

It would be my closest time with Gaston. Everything else fell away; we were up to our elbows in words. Our mutual master. But what the process revealed was how different our relation to words actually was. What a poet does in French, I began to realize, is profoundly unlike what a poet does in English. Their experience of language is not the same. Or at least we discovered a gulf of that kind, and in the end we couldn't bridge it.

We sat at a big table in the dining room, books and drafts spread out, and worked through the translation line by line.

Marc was not a poet himself, and Gaston had many improvements to suggest: tactfully, but firmly. His grasp of the poems' content was glorious — far better than many English speakers'. I was at home in the discussion, though out of my depth when it came to nuances in French.

But we kept getting stuck. It was mostly with turns of phrase where I'd bent the English, played words off each other in an improvisational way that was strange even to English-speakers, but that got something said I couldn't articulate any other way. And all I could steer by, for validation of the unfamiliar music, was that tiny, irrefutable *ping!* that goes off, sometimes on the fiftieth draft, when the words finally click into place.

After a lot of back-and-forthing with me, Marc had done his best to recreate this linguistic new-mintedness in French. But now, to my consternation, Gaston kept blocking his attempts. I wish I could cite some examples, but the drafts are long gone. All I have now is the memory of Gaston reaching for his big *Robert* dictionary, yet again, with grave, implacable courtesy, to see if the vapour trail of nuance which Lebel was trying to bring across from English was listed among the seventeen meanings of whatever French word Marc had chosen. If the twelfth entry for the word included the connotation Marc was looking for, the word stayed in. If not, it was toast.

I sat there flummoxed. What did this deference to the dictionary have to do with poetry?

I got a crash course in poetics that weekend — in French and in English. I found myself parading around the room, delivering fireball manifestos I never knew I espoused (especially in the Alice-in-Wonderland French they emerged in). Okay, I declared: taking them individually, I couldn't judge how the attempts to recreate my unexpected English were working. I didn't know how many of them emitted that unmistakable *ping!* in French. But taking the sequence as a whole, you couldn't just standardize the language, plane it down, make it correct. (Jeez: did this sound like a defence of bad grammar? Sloppy diction?) The English wasn't "correct." It bounced through a dozen vocal registers, from slang to metaphysics, playing their musics against each other. You had cello, you had sax, you had kazoo. (I was hitting my stride now.) The poem wasn't just about its content — it was a chancy trek through language itself. And sometimes, though barely, an arrival at the unknown speech of my undiscovered country. (*Yes!* The wild WASP in flight!) The reason its noises were so unfamiliar was that I was just learning to write Canadian. But if I followed words for real, I had to let them take me any-vocal-where they wanted. There was no safety net. (*Go! Go!*) And to screen out that dimension of verbal play was to geld the voices I'd been claimed by — to turn me into one more colonial sub-Englishman, one more wannabe-American. (Yikes: this was getting out of hand. Did I really think Gaston Miron was a Yankee imperialist?)

There was a good deal more, which I won't go into here. The genius of English poetry since Chaucer, I declared, has drawn on a language perpetually in process — made new, getting born and reborn in the very instant the words hit the page. To tap into that process of "jail-break and re-creation," as Margaret Avison puts it, is to join a line of descent which includes Shakespeare, Milton, Whitman, Hopkins, Pound. And which now includes whatever we do in the ex-colonies, as we finally emerge into our unknown voices. If we can manage to get struck by lightning. ...

Gaston listened to my highwire orating, with that huge innate courtesy, and went back to correcting Marc's French.

◆

I was ready to weep with frustration and baffled affection. And throughout the rest of the weekend, I never figured out what was going on. All I knew was that the deep affinity which Miron and Lee had discovered was no longer there; not, at least, when we reached the heart of what claimed us both — the ache and resonance of words. We came from different planets.

Eighteen years later, I can see the bigger picture. I know that "Miron" doesn't equal "all poets who write in French"; I shouldn't generalize just from him. I can also conjecture that his resistance to unconventional usage was of a piece with his refusal of *joual* as a literary medium. And that prompts a deeper realization: the point is not just what Miron was against (*joual*, harum-scarum linguistic innovation), but what he was *for*.

His relation to language was profoundly conservative. And so was mine. But what we were conserving was two different things. When Gaston turned to *Robert* for guidance, he wasn't being a fussy reactionary. He was reaching back into a living tradition, probing to see if these johnny-come-lately turns of phrase might legitimately extend it. I may never be fully at home with what that tradition finds sacred: a penetration to essence, a purity of expression which knows about the contingent, but refuses to wallow in it. (Have I said this without caricature?)

For my part, when I assumed that English is up for grabs each time I sit down with a blank piece of paper — that its very nature is to enact both essence and flux — I too was honouring the tradition I was born in. I was being equally conservative. But the integrity of each tradition was its own; the genius of one was not the genius of the other.

And neither could I assume that I was a special case. Miron's relation to language was not something to plea-bargain with. Even if he loved the poems; even if he cared about me. The craggy integrity that led him to publish *Civil Elegies* when he might be trashed for doing so was the same integrity that now insisted on historically proper French. His life project was of a piece; I either accepted both forms of integrity, or I accepted neither. ... Of course, I accepted both.

So there we were: three men in a house in Quebec, doing our best at a quixotic project, for no other reason than that it was worth doing. And we were going to fail. There were realities our goodwill and mutual respect couldn't conjure out of existence.

At the functional level, we got the job done. Late Sunday evening, we drove back to Montreal. And the translation appeared in 1980.

◆

I have a few more Mirons in memory. The book was launched at a reading with Gaston and Paul Chamberland — was that in Quebec City? — and we were back in sync again. We had a ball. And later in the '80s, we sat down together a few more times in Montreal. There was a palpable sadness in Gaston now, but the courtesy was still unfailing. And that uncanny mix of *spoudaios*, high seriousness, with sheer verve of being: that still prevailed. He gave me a copy of his slim collection *Courtepointes*, inscribed — have I got it right? my copy isn't here — "Ces deux nations, nous les créerons ensemble." Fraternal independence.

I loved this man. And what I come to finally is a poem I wrote two years ago. I never thought it would stand as goodbye to Miron.

Tell the Ones You Love

Tell the ones you love, you
love them;
tell them now.
For the day is coming, and also the night will come,
when you will neither say it, nor hear it, nor care.
Tell the ones you love.
I have lost many who mattered, and I will say it again:
tell the ones you love, you love them.
Tell them today.

Part III

The Luminous Tumult:
Finding the Structure of *Riffs*

Suppose you're writing a longish poem — let's say it's a sequence. You want it to move from one state of affairs at the beginning to a different state at the end. But there's no story to supply the forward momentum, so you need a trajectory of some other kind.

And that's where you're stymied. You've got a stockpile of loosely connected poems — but they don't have a common through-line, to propel the sequence ahead.

That dilemma kept nagging at me, all through the 1980s, in a sequence called Riffs. *Eventually it would settle down as a suite of eighty-eight short lyrics, depicting a bumpy love affair. But before that happened, I accumulated some 1,500 poems — with no idea what the overall shape should be. It took me ten years to figure that out. And when I did, the solution was so obvious that my misbegotten attempts seemed almost comical.*

The following dialogue is based on an interview with Russell Brown and Donna Bennett, savvy critics and editors, who had witnessed the search for the phantom structure in the early years.

Dennis, you published an interim version of Riffs *in 1982 — eleven years ago. And the finished sequence has just appeared. That's a pretty long gestation period, even for you. I'm interested in what you were wrestling with.*

During most of that time, I couldn't see what the structure of the sequence should be. Actually, I didn't know what *kind* of a sequence it should be.

Can you talk about that? I mean, the concrete issues of craft. For instance, you'd already written two long poems, Civil Elegies *and* The Death of Harold Ladoo. *Were they any help?*

Oh no. Apart from the business of orchestrating different voices, they were no help at all. Almost the opposite.

So how did Riffs *begin?*

With a kind of vocal meltdown.

Meaning …?

It was only the second time in my life that a new voice had arrived out of the blue. It happened with *Civil Elegies*. And it happened again with this much jazzier voice, in the winter and spring of '81. About a thousand of these little pieces came through in a couple of months.

My personal life was pretty fraught at the time, that was part of it. I was living in Edinburgh, on the Canada-Scotland exchange — away from distractions here, so I had high hopes for writing. But I wasted months on a long poem that went nowhere, I wrote the polyphony essay, and that was that. And my marriage broke up at Christmas.

So I was sitting up every night in the apartment, drinking too much and picking scabs.

And then around March, these *things* began. I remember the first night. I had the headphones on, playing some Buddy Holly, and I started doing a kind of automatic writing. About a love affair I'd gotten into, which was on hold because the woman had gone away for a month. It came in quick little stings; I'd scribble one down, draw a line, start the next. And the voice kept jumping around, all these honks and bleats and weird unofficial music. It was just noodling, though. I had no idea I was starting *Riffs*.

Anyway, I got up the next morning and found thirty-five of these things. Most of them were therapeutic junk, but a couple had a funny quality I didn't recognize — one of them started:

> Home-spooked
> hotline.   Nobody's li'l number
>
> one.   Big-eyed
> radium child on stretched-out scrims of alert — ...

Now, something like that coming out of your pen can get your attention. I know it got mine. Here I was, a meditative poet who did long, ruminative, publicly resonant things — I had a perfectly decent way of writing already. What was *this*? But the next night I tried again, and along with the crud I got a few more with that bizarre crackle and pop.

Still about the love affair?

Still about the love affair — or the lack of it. So it became the thing I did at night. Pretty soon there were hundreds and hundreds of them — maybe a thousand — in this whole marching band of voices. They could sound like this:

Wal, acey deucey
    trey divide —
I'm a guy with a fine wide-eyed

lady freckles too &
    squirms when she
feels good ...

Or like this:

Am going soon, but meanwhile I can hear
what mortals care for,
instep and desire.
Tell me what you cherish, won't
just walk; give me lifetime,
not renege ...

Or this:

Blood on
    behemoth.

Tracts of sheer
    unness.

Abyss and
    interludes.
I did that thing, I just can't walk home straight.

And on and on it went, night after night. With the voices going all over the map. And you've got to understand: in the late '70s, I'd been writing one or two short poems a year — none of them remotely like this.

Who else was writing this way? "Unofficial music," you called it. In these little blurts, with the influence from jazz and rock and blues, and with literary decorum out the window. It seems like a very North American mode.

It is. But I hadn't seen a whole lot of it even here. This kind of music — it's not the same thing as the conversational voice you hear in so much North American poetry. It can draw on vernacular and slang, but it's really about the process of vocal improvisation itself; that, and the pulse of feeling. It's a riffy, iffy, intuitive thing. Individual pieces are often lightweight in content, but the music itself makes the real declaration.

But what did you do with these improvisations? It's now the late spring of '81, and you've written a thousand of them.

Well, by summer the affair was over, and I was back in Toronto. And the nightly flood was over too; it had lasted three or four months. There were maybe a hundred pieces I could see working with. It got as far as the version that appeared in *Descant* in 1982 — which you helped me structure, Donna. But it still hadn't gelled. Far from it. And the various attempts I made in the years after that didn't get much further.

So it's been a two-stage process. First, the arrival in this chariots-of-fire fashion, with a rough shaping. And then ten more years, while I tried to figure out what I had on my hands. I wrote another five hundred pieces along the way, but I didn't get the whole thing right till last year. Once it fell into place, it was hard to see why it had taken so long.

Just to complete the picture: I started a second sequence, "Nightwatch," in 1985. It's been my co-albatross, along with *Riffs* — for a while I thought they might be a single long poem. So for eight years, both sequences have been on the go.

Looking at the final shape of Riffs, *I'm struck by the fact that it* is *a* sequence, *rather than a continuous long poem like* Ladoo. *The way you've described its evolution, this seems like the appropriate form for it to take. Could you talk about how you shaped it?*

The first thing is that it came in these little spurts of improvisation. Intense, close up, with the emotional and linguistic experience going *splat* on the page. They really are riffs, which by definition are quickies.

I presume people know what a riff is. The word comes from jazz, and it refers to one of those little melodic improvisations a soloist does. Though strange to say, back in the swing era, in the 1930s, a riff was when the gentlemen in the brass section stood up and went, "Wah-WAAAH, wah ... Wah-WAAAH, wah ..." And then the soloist would improvise: "Da-zingo, *snick*! / Zoom, gobble-da-gobble-da / Wacko doo-dah-*dit* / And the price of fish!" — all that in five or six seconds. And then the riff brigade starts up again: "Wah-WAAAH, wah ..." The latter being basically rhythmic, with no melodic interest and no particular feeling. And scored in advance, of course, since everybody had to play the same thing. ... Anyway, that's what a riff was in the '30s. But by the kind of transfer where "Frankenstein" went from being the mad scientist to the monster, "riff" went from being the rhythmic filler to the solo fireworks.

So these things came through as riffs, in the solo sense. But that made the question of structuring them hard to deal with. Emotionally, the focal length was about a hundredth of an inch. The pieces have almost no distance on the experience they're about; at their riffiest, they aren't *about* an experience at all — they *are* the experience. Often there's no paraphrasable content. And that confused me. The fact that they relied on voice — that much I was at home with. But my adult stuff had always had heavy-duty content too, and these sure didn't. What on earth is the "content" of something like this?

> SKID skid, dopey li'l
> juggernaut;
> Molotov sidecar momma, wrench me a frog.
>
> If you got happiness tablets throw some out the window way down opposite side.

There's just this feeling of revved-up emptiness, and the vamping in words.

If there wasn't much content to steer by, how did *you organize them?*

That was the big question. At first I hoped the vocal trajectory itself would tell the story. There weren't many themes — as in musical themes. Boy gets girl, feels good; boy loses girl, sucks thumb. That was about it. So I hoped you could take that for granted, and concentrate on the tonal changes; you'd hear the shifts from voice to voice tracing out the emotional progression — from goofy to sad to grave, and on and on. But it didn't work. After you'd read a couple of dozen of these things, you just went into a trance; there was no sense of forward movement at all.

Which made me question some of my ideas about polyphony (right after I'd written the essay about it, of course). Was it really enough on its own? Those first runs at organizing *Riffs* were pretty uncompromising, the way they took shifts of voice as the only structural guide. It wasn't surprising that some people I showed it to couldn't connect; the voices were weird. But even readers who liked the noises — myself, for a start — got bogged down. It seemed as if an extended sequence, at least when it was made up of so many short pieces, needed more than just a polyphonic trajectory to hold it together. Only with these things, what else *was* there?

What else did you try?

I was stymied. I never thought of turning them into a continuous poem — with no section breaks, I mean — but I must have tried every other wrong-headed possibility. That first version in *Descant*, for instance: it had a narrative line of sorts, but I had to spell it out in prose at the beginning, which was far too mechanical.

The problem was, I was trying to tell a story in a series of quick takes. And while each take could give you a single, stop-time moment, that seemed to scotch the possibility of a continuous story. The speaker's wigged-out consciousness wasn't available for orderly narration, that's for sure. Not credibly. But if you tried to shift into the third person — so you could move around, set the scene, all that narrative stuff — you undercut the main voice. If we're going to go with *that* voice, with its strung-out intensity, there can't be some other, more matter-of-fact intelligence at the same time, efficiently stage-managing things. It would make the juiced-up voice seem like a curio on display, and we wouldn't join in. Or so it seemed to me.

Poe was the first person to talk about this stuff. And what he said was, Screw the creaky narrative machinery; just go for the quick, lyric intensity. A long narrative poem, with all the paraphernalia you have to include, is a non-starter. Don't waste your time trying. And that's the dilemma I was stuck in. I wanted more than just a songbook, but I couldn't find a satisfactory formal logic for the whole thing.

What about your interest in jazz? Did it give you any leads? ... Let me frame that another way. Would you call yourself a jazz poet? In Riffs, *I mean?*

Not necessarily. I'd call it jazz poetry; it stands or falls by the sense of improvisation. But whether or not the only way to get that is by literally improvising — which means, using only first drafts — that's a separate question. A first draft may have exactly the right quicksilver moves, and I'm chuffed when it does. But if the fiftieth draft has more of that white-hot feeling, of the words coming into existence just as they hit the page, that's the one I go with. The experience on the page is what counts; the way you achieve it is irrelevant. So I was always prepared to revise.

Language just isn't the same medium as pure rhythm and sound — you're dealing with meaning as well. And that makes it a different animal. Sometimes with a poem you have to revise your way toward improv.

But jazz has been important in your writing, hasn't it?

Jazz has been my biggest influence in the last decade. Even though it didn't kick in seriously till after that spring in Edinburgh, believe it or not. The improvisational leads I was following back then came from abstract expressionism — aka action painting, which is indicative — and some stray remarks of Charles Olson's.

Let me clarify this. I don't mean "jazz influence" the way you find it in Beat poetry, where you caught some live music, and tried to recreate the way it made you feel: you went on about the searing purple of the orgasmic sax, and the writing itself was pretty purple. Those folk may have loved jazz, but they didn't know enough about poetry. So I don't take jazz as the subject matter. Nor as a program you try to imitate in words. Occasionally in *Riffs* there are musical references — you'll hear a phrase from the blues, or a little run of polly-wolly-doodle. But that's just local kibitzing; it's not the kind of subterranean influence we're talking about.

It's partly the spur-of-the-moment *form* that kills me in jazz: the way the melodic shape conjures itself out of nowhere. And also the exploration of pure feeling. In older recorded jazz they had two or three minutes to work in, and they moved so fast, into such an intensity of emotion. Straight to the bloodstream! Look at those solos by — oh, whoever: the sax is what speaks to me most, so Parker, Ben Webster, Lester Young. Small-group stuff, before the LP changed everything. Especially bop. There's a couple of lead-in bars — and hang on, there you are inside this pure ache or exultation as it finds its shape, flowering out of its own insides but also part of what the whole group is doing with some old sock of a theme — and then, *wham*! it's over. That kind of magic, my body just feels at home in. It's had as much effect on my recent poetry as anything I read in words — often I miss that fireball grace in literature.

But still, the affinity there is with individual riffs. It didn't help with the shape of the whole sequence.

The music I hear in your poetry, particularly Riffs, *exists at the level of rhythm and syncopation. Something is going on in the line that's similar to jazz.*

It's particularly the phrasing. In *Riffs* it comes in bites; sometimes there's a long arching line, but it always unfolds *after* a series of quick nips or swoops. There's a sense of pounce, of staccato phrasing — I can talk about it better with body English than I can in words.

That prosody opened up while I was working on *Riffs*. Previously, I'd gravitated to a long tumbling line. With a cross-tension set up by the line breaks, and by syntactic splaying within the sentences. But with *Riffs*, I heard a different kind of rhythm. To catch it, you need to feel the underlying energy, the cadence, muscling up through the words and propelling the piece ahead. It may be easier to hear if you set the two rhythmic idioms side by side. It's the difference between how the energy moved in *Civil Elegies*, say —

> Often I sit in the sun and brooding over the city, always
> in airborne shapes among the pollution I hear them, returning;

> pouring across the square
> in fetid descent they darken the towers
> and the wind-swept place of meeting, and whenever
> the thick air clogs my breathing it teems with their presence ...

— and the way it moves in *Riffs*. For instance:

> Hey, should I
> talk
> sociology?
>
> when where what how who?
>
> All I
> want, woman, is
> crawl up your left nostril & snuff it for keeps in sexual asthma heaven.

You can feel the difference in the two kinds of locomotion, right? And plugging into this edgier way of moving was part of the electricity.

Was that connected with your sense of improvisation?

Absolutely.

But how can you sustain that with a poem you've worked on for so long? ... Trick question.

But a good one, believe me. It would have been easy to lose the spur-of-the-moment feel, when I kept on revising. Particularly because the pieces I've written in the last couple of years, which coaxed this final shape out of the sequence — a number of them are more poems than riffs. And in a poem, you're working with a different kind of consciousness, more self-aware. The sequence needed that, so I wasn't just shooting everything in close-up. But finding out how to move from riffs to poems to riffs again, without wrecking the fabric of the whole thing: that was crucial.

Not everything in the book is a riff, in the sense I'm talking about. Some of them, I don't know *what* they are, and maybe they're the purest riffs. They were the scariest. But some of the recent ones are recognizably poems. If you nailed me to the wall and said, name the three characteristics that distinguish a riff from a poem, I probably couldn't. But as the guy who wrote the thing, I know there's a difference.

Was there a difference in the way you wrote them?

Definitely. The riffs began with a pell-mell first draft; the poems came a few lines at a time, like my previous stuff. The riffs were harder to do, because I had to disconnect my brain. And when the full-tilt-boogie improv was happening, it felt as if there was this whole flux of pre-meaning; there was a groundswell of dangerous energy, and the words bubbled up from it. The improvisation depended on walking into it and getting hit from all sides. Even if you might change some of the words later on.

If you just sit down and analyze a riff, you're likely to get this wrong. You can dissect the wordplay, say, the riffle-shuffle of meanings — and fair enough, that's part of the spoor of the energy. But you're starting from the wrong end, if you give "meaning" precedence over the luminous tumult it rises out of. The pre-verbal cadence. That's what sweeps you along, not just the twiddles and hiccups of meaning. And if *Riffs* is erotic, it's because that energy is — not simply because some of the pieces talk about making love.

Along with explosions of individual riffs, the sequence explodes a personal relationship. Are those things related?

Well, yes and no. Let me talk about the personal element first. The pieces did begin in a real affair, and for several years I kept pretty close to what actually happened. But that was naive. It was only when I started attending to the affair on the page that I found my way ahead. And then it could go anywhere. So if you treat it as a documentary episode from the author's life, you miss the basic point. What matters is the emotional truth it's exploring. Along with the music, of course.

But there's one real-life thing I didn't tamper with, and *Riffs* could hardly exist without it. The guy in the book has this whirligig romance, the woman goes away, and he starts these nightly sessions. But words are the only thing he's got now, words and scotch whisky, so words are where the lightning has to strike. The riffs themselves become the erotic fix. The surrogate ecstasy.

Now, that had been my own experience in 1981 — of reactivating the "sheer valhalla overdrive" in words. And without my even realizing it, that became the central convention of *Riffs*. The guy is making his nightly grab at glory, scratching the numinous itch. Over and over, till it becomes an addiction. Because one thing the sequence is doing is trying to improvise a connection with the sacred. Whatever that might consist of, when the old ways of connecting have been shut down.

But this creates a weird circularity. You know? Each riff is a finished object — but at the same time, it's a gesture. An action. A pass at one more high in words. The act of cruising for one more riff — that *is* the present-tense plot. ... Though with a certain brittleness, I'd say. This is electroshock loving, not the deep resilience of two lives over decades. And it's a large burden to lay on one little affair. In fact, on writing itself. It's a form of idolatry. That way burnout lies, and eventually the sequence has to mime the sound of his nervous system crashing. ... But my job was to track those things, not to make the guy live more sensibly.

Anyway, that's a formal strategy I could never have arrived at by planning. It came straight out of the original experience. Even calling it a "strategy" seems a bit wrong-headed, since it was such a mix of lunacy and luck. But it supplies much of the underpinning for *Riffs* as a dramatic poem.

When you speak of it this way, I wonder why you felt it needed any further continuity. Beyond this improvisational quest by the speaker, what were you after?

You do these things in the dark. When I was dissatisfied all through the '80s, I couldn't say why it felt unfinished. It just *did*. I wanted something you'd read both ways: as a sequence in ecstatic form, *and* in linear form. But I couldn't see how to manage it. ... I remember rereading the *Dream Songs*, to see what Berryman had done. But even though I loved individual pieces, the sequence as a whole wasn't any help, because as a sequence it doesn't gel. In the first installment, Berryman had this tenuous hook he hoped would give it some coherence — the Henry/Mr. Bones routine. But that peters out. And eventually the songs just accumulate, to the point that all 385 are a lesser whole than thirty or forty of them. Going back to it confirmed my sense that a batch of bare naked riffs was always going to be just that. A batch. A miscellany. A sequence needed more linear purchase than he'd located, more forward momentum. Or equally to the point, more than I had.

I also went back to *Maud*, which I remembered as having some killer lyrics *and* a storyline. But the whole thing was sandbagged by a different problem, which I hadn't solved in *Riffs* either. It started whenever I tried to give my speaker a daily life where things actually happened — which is one of the approaches I experimented with. But how was he supposed to trot out some brisk reportage on the day's events, considering the state he was in? And anyway, it wouldn't have taken. I winced at the way the speaker in *Maud* has to narrate the plot — there's nobody else around for the job. But his credibility flies out the window. All you're aware of is Tennyson forcing the poor sod to recount events to people who just went through the events *with* him, earlier the same day. It's not believable, it throws you right out of the poem. ... And the problem goes deeper. The speaker in *Maud* is wingy, living on the edge, and that's where the lyric energy comes from — like in that eerie piece where he imagines himself dead, with feet tramping over his head. But the fact is, that voice doesn't belong in workaday, linear time. The pure ecstatic moment, even if it's pure ecstatic despair, is the only place it's at home. So the plot poems clank like Halloween skeletons. They're just not good poetry, they come from Tennyson's superego. His heart wasn't in it, and it shows. They're doing what Poe criticized long poems for, wedging in structural stuff that puts us to sleep. ... All of which was painfully evident in my own drafts. Poe was wrong about the *Iliad*, but he was right about *Riffs* — at least, when I tried to make it tell a story about daily events.

But you still haven't told us what you did *do. How you finally got it to work.*

I won't go on about the rest of the things I tried; they could stand as a survey of how to botch a lyric sequence. And don't forget: for a while, I was trying to combine *Riffs* and "Nightwatch" — the second sequence I'd started. Which just made things worse.

Anyway, the move that finally took didn't involve a new formal approach at all. It simply meant changing one detail — making the woman married. It sounds absurd, but that brought the whole sequence into sync with itself.

I'd always been bugged by the question, why don't these two get back together? If the guy is missing her so much, why doesn't he just go see her? (The autobiographical reason, that their lives lay on different continents, was no use in the poem.) But once I gave her a husband, things fell into place.

At the simplest level, it explained the block in their affair. Now the woman could be away on a trip with her husband, trying to decide whether to stay with him or leave him for her lover, the guy who's speaking in *Riffs*. Plus, now the story didn't have to include a lot of new events. It could rely on discovering that things we'd read near the beginning were not as we thought. This never *was* an innocent love affair. So you could have a backward-leaning, forward-tilting narrative — revelations about the past would propel the present ahead. This was hardly news in fiction, but it wasn't something I'd seen in lyric poetry. And I liked the formal effect. As you read, you could go mainly with the stop-time riffs; or you could let the emerging backstory define the shape of things; or you could do both.

And now the polyphony, the trajectory of voices, could enact the emotional flow more cleanly. Once it wasn't being asked to carry the structural load all by itself. And so the deeper currents of feeling could start to animate the sequence. I haven't said much about them, but I imagine they're obvious: the hunger, the shame, the sense of sterner moral necessities, the cold-turkey withdrawal from this big emotional jag.

It's a funny thing. You're working with an energy that isn't literally on the page, but it has to breathe life into the whole poem. It's like trying to open a space for the wind to blow through. The words are just the track of its going, they're not the energy itself. I find this one of the most mysterious things in writing an extended poem. The most important thing you're working with is never actually on the page.

Did it do anything else, making the woman married?

Well, it seemed to resolve the problem of credibility. It may be an unwelcome fact that somebody whose lover is married will airbrush that commitment — unconsciously wish it away. But while that may be reprehensible, it doesn't strain our belief. So for the speaker not to mention a husband for half the sequence, and then lurch into flagellating himself about it — that felt realistic.

And it went a step further. The speaker has had access to eros central; and we believe it, I think, because of the accents of runaway ecstasy in his voice. But when it develops that it's all been triggered by a season of tacky adultery — what are we to make of *that*? I loved the artistic leverage it gave on quandaries of good and bad. It opened into uncomfortable mysteries I'm gripped by. And now I could explore them straight-on, without constantly tripping over technical difficulties that weren't germane.

I scarcely realized it at first, but making the woman married allowed a clean, invisible economy across the whole sequence. It made *Riffs* finishable. So with some help from my wife and friends, and the excellent editor at *Brick*, I finished it.

Poetry as a Mongrel Medium

When it last appeared in public, back in 1998, this essay was titled "Poetry and Unknowing." And it was three times as long as it is here. There's a story behind its dramatic weight loss.

When I wrote it, I was in my mid-fifties, and I had decided to start meditating. I was a novice. But I sat for fifteen minutes each day, letting go of distractions as best I could, and breathing in time with a phrase I'd taken as my mantra: "Thank you." I wasn't thanking any specific you; I just wanted to centre down in the gratitude and awe I felt at being alive. To "worship without belief," as I phrased it to myself.

I stayed with that modest practice for a year, and during this time I wrote "Poetry and Unknowing." There I explored the devotional practice known as the negative way, aka the dark night of the soul, aka the cloud of unknowing. That is, I explored it at second hand, based on my reading. For decades I'd been fascinated by the masters of this tradition, like Meister Eckhart, St. John of the Cross, the anonymous author of The Cloud. *They taught the discipline of "naughting" — where a member of a contemplative community found him or herself being pried loose from standard religious beliefs and consolations, which (they realized) they'd been using for their own comfort and benefit. It was a summons to go beyond spiritual materialism, often with severe withdrawal pangs, as they relinquished everything that appeared to constitute religion. It was extreme purification.*

Could there be any kind of fit, I wondered, between that practice and meditation in a secular era — where for many people, such as myself, traditional belief is no longer possible? The discipline in both cases was to wait in emptiness, letting go of affirmative content, with no expectation.

Needless to say, there was an immense gulf between these masters and my kindergarten meditation. Still, in poetry I had almost thirty years' experience of letting go — ceding the initiative to cadence. Maybe that discipline was relevant in meditation, as a lesser version of the negative way. Maybe it was transferable?

After a year, I took stock. And what struck me was the difference between my experience with cadence and my experience in meditation. For instance:

- *When I hunkered down in cadence, I wasn't waiting for some exotic unknown process to begin. Cadence was there before I was — very alive, very matter of fact. With myself, by happenstance, embedded in it. But I experienced nothing comparable to that during my meditation sessions. So "affirmative content" wasn't being* withdrawn *from me, as it was in the negative way — affirmative content had never begun in the first place. There was nothing in my meditative life to be naughted.*
- *It took no effort of will for me to wait on cadence, even at times when the connection was faint. If anything, it took greater willpower to step* away *from it, to re-enter the daily flow of the household. In meditation, by contrast, I had to work hard to stay blank and receptive for even fifteen minutes. I was in my native element in mode cadence, and I was a visiting outsider in mode meditation.*

So I gave up meditating, and concentrated solely on cadence again. I didn't dismiss the reality of meditation. But I was in my fifties, time was ticking, and I had learned something at first hand. Poetry was a deep practice that was already open to me; meditation was not. That bruised my self-regard for a spell, but it clarified things. I'd taken a detour, a grandiose one, and it was time to re-focus.

For this appearance of "Poetry and Unknowing," I've stripped away the would-be-mystical pensées that took over the mic last time. In their place, I've expanded on what was a secondary motif: the "mongrel medium" I relied on while I was writing The Death of Harold Ladoo.

Ladoo was an intense, gifted, complex Trinidadian I knew in Toronto — the author of a short and searing novel, No Pain Like This Body. *I had edited it with him. He was murdered in 1973, at age twenty-eight. And writing the elegy for him had taught me a lot about the kind of meditating I'm actually equipped to practise. That's what I investigate here.*

Dennis, you've been called a philosophical poet. Is that accurate?

As a first approximation, maybe. But if you look at how philosophers think, and how poets think, they're two different animals.

How so?

Well, let me sketch some background. As you know, there's more than one type of thinking. And the kind that interests me most is *gestalt* thinking. Where you're faced with a batch of apparently unrelated details, in whatever field. Or across several fields. But you have a hunch that there's a pattern. You're hoping for that "Ah-*hah*!" moment, when the details suddenly click into focus together. They're no longer a ragbag — they *cohere*. But as we know from experience: sometimes you do discern such a gestalt, and sometimes you don't. There's no guarantee.

Okay, back to your question. People practise gestalt thinking in both philosophy and poetry. But in most philosophy I know, it's purely cerebral. Yes, the philosopher can discern an unfamiliar pattern. But only if it can be expressed in verbal terms, and in fact in logical terms. If there's a gestalt of some other *kind*, it will remain off the radar. Or else they'll patronize it — treat it as a failed attempt at rational thinking.

I see what you're getting at in philosophy. But what about gestalt thinking in poetry? And specifically, in your work?

Well, the longish poems I write — the ones I call meditations — are searching for gestalt coherence, no question. But they have their own way of searching, and they need a more mongrel medium than pure reasoning is comfortable with. A poetic meditation draws on a whole range of resources — on the rational mind, certainly, but also on body rhythms and movements of the heart and communal memory and busted myths and curious anecdotes and who-knows-what-all. It has to advance on all these wavelengths at once. And often, on top of that, a meditation aims to *exemplify* the gestalt it's seeking — not just wax on about it.

It's taken me years to sort this out. When I first launched into gestalt thinking in poetry, I could sometimes *do* it, but I had no idea what it was I was doing.

Why didn't you write meditations from the start?

I kind of got delayed. It boggles me now, but my first book consisted of sonnets and sonnet variations. Which was precisely what I didn't need — a short, pre-set structure to work in. It meant that the lope and sprawl and exploratory improv that are intrinsic to meditation had no room to breathe, to stretch out and sniff around.

Which leads me to *voice* — voice as the medium for gestalt thinking. Sometimes I think I'm an idolater of voice. And to speak in shorthand: a voice doesn't just state — it *embodies*. A given tonality resonates with a certain frequency in the way things are — and if it rings true, you sense that frequency vibrating across the length and breadth of what-is. It permits a kind of sonic mapping, a kinesthetic probe. So it's a natural medium for gestalt reconnaissance.

What's more, a poem can be *polyphonic*. It can move from one voice to another. So for me, at least, a meditation doesn't just trundle from content A to content B to content C in a single voice. Philosophical thinking proceeds that way. But in a meditative poem, there are all these vocal shifts, and they enact successive stages in the exploration — first embodying *this* content in *this* voice; then idling sideways to embody new content in another voice; then spurting ahead to a third inflection. Moving in the free-form way we do when we're tracking something with our whole lives. And that vocal trek itself constitutes a coherent mode of thinking, a distinct form of knowing. Where voice *embodies*, and polyphony *enacts*.

So voice *and* polyphony *are key elements in your poetics. Another is* cadence. *And you've talked about how hard it is to define what the word refers to.*

I experience it all the time, but I still get tongue-tied. "Cadence" is my term for the flux of energies I sense — the felt and living flux that poems arise from. It's where the voices teem — it *is* the voices, intuited first without words. Only how do you talk about that, when talking depends *on* it?

Not that talking about it is the point. Months or years can go by, and I don't think once about cadence — not as a separate object of enquiry. All I'm trying to do is let some words move on the page the way they want to. Like — why is there such a lurch in the middle of page three, when it moves from one section to the next? It doesn't feel right, and eventually I realize — the second section doesn't belong in the poem at all. So out it goes. And then a month passes and I think, well, there's one little run in the cancelled chunk that might work, if we segued into it over here — which is two pages further on. So I try it there. ... You know? You're trying to do justice to the way something wants to move. You don't know what the something is: you don't know what the kinetic shape of it should be; you're just mucking about in the middle, trying to follow the lines of force. It's intuitive, and it's cadence that guides you.

This mucking about seems to involve a great deal of revision. How does that work?

Well, let's get concrete. Think of *The Death of Harold Ladoo*, the way it probes for a deeper and deeper gestalt. Harold was murdered in 1973, and for months I wanted to write an elegy. And eventually some stuff started coming through; it led to the two italicized passages in the finished poem, which address Ladoo in this elevated tone. One of them starts, "*Great raging maker, Ladoo: go dead and legendary / in permanent regions of praise ...*" When I wrote those lines, it seemed as if they were the whole poem. I played with the passage that first day — there were about fifteen lines, which seemed almost enough — but when I came back the next day, it wasn't quite there yet. So I tweaked it a bit ... and a bit more ... and away we went. It took a year and a half, and ended up maybe 750 lines long.

And as it expanded, I found myself dealing with a funny process of recoil, kickback, argumentation with a normal high-style elegy. Because there was a certain dishonesty in that first draft, where Harold is "dead and legendary" — *full stop*. Case closed. There was nothing untrue in the praise, but it sure papered over a lot of complexities in his life and writing. And I didn't know what to do about that — until I realized, the complexities could be included right on the page. So I started breaking taboos, exploring things that qualified and undercut and painted moustaches on the Mona Lisa of a traditional elegy. The discordant stuff didn't even feel like poetry. But releasing it into words, letting it break through in a series of jagged pendulum swings — that became the structural basis of the whole poem. With each new energy jolt hijacking the poem for a spell, but then getting integrated into the ongoing meditation. And with these successive movements serving as the basic units, the building-blocks, in the gestalt which the poem was searching for.

Here's the speaker's first recoil, where he blurts out a savage counter-truth to the initial praise. His feelings are raw, and the voice is pretty raw too:

> And as for you Ladoo — you never missed a trick.
> You soaked up love like a sponge. ...
> You had us taped, you knew white
> liberals inside out: how to
> guilt us; which buttons to push; how hard; how long.
> ...
> Ladoo, you bastard, goodbye: you bled me dry.
> You used me! and though the words are
> not what I intended, they rankle but let me get them said:
> goodbye, and good riddance.

And that's just the beginning. The speaker goes through a whole series of hairpin swerves — each bringing one more partial truth into the open. Here he implicates himself:

> But make no mistake, Ladoo:
> I was devouring you too, in the overall
> carnage and we did feed off each other,
> you gave your blood at last.
> I needed you to be the thing of fantasy
> I now detest, as also I detest
> the shoddy yen in myself. ...
> Say it: I used you, Harold,
> like a hypocrite voyeur.

Across the whole poem, there are six or eight of these revisionist perspectives on Ladoo; they're not always tidily demarcated, so it's hard to be precise. Plus, I've been tracing only the speaker's individual, one-on-one relation to Ladoo. But the poem goes on to set that in a much broader context: the erosion of a sacramental universe, and the revenge of the exiled gods.

Anyway, here's how things conclude, near the end of the elegy. You can sense how the poem's weathered voice has absorbed all the contradictory energies that boiled up en route. For instance, how the whiplash, line-to-line rhythm finally stabilizes — with most of the lines now end-stopped (whether we notice it consciously or not). And so the complex ritual of grieving — which is the deep gestalt the poem has been making its way through — prepares to wind down:

> I read these words and flinch, for I had not meant
> to quarrel with you, Harold.
> Nor with friends, good men and women, who also lived these things.
> Nor with myself.
> Though I feel nothing for you
> I did not feel before your death,
> I loved you, and I owed you words of my own.
> But speaking the words out loud has brought me close to the bone.

To return to your original point — yes, the poems go through a lot of revision. And it doesn't necessarily stop when a piece gets published. Once *Ladoo* appeared to be finished, in 1976, Robert Bringhurst offered to publish it at Kanchenjunga Press — in time for a reading I was giving in Vancouver. He stayed up all night the night before, collating and stitching this handsome chapbook. But I had already revised the version I'd sent him a few weeks earlier. So at the event, he's standing at the back of the hall when I start to read — and suddenly he snatches up a copy and goes riffling through it. "What the hell is Lee reading? I don't remember this part at all!"

So this is by way of saying: there are different kinds of thinking, different ways of knowing. Logical reasoning is one way — and long may it flourish, within its boundaries. But most people call on a richer, more whichway array of resources when they're exploring something that matters to them. I gravitate to poetry that thinks in this mongrel way.

Body Music:
Notes on Micro-Rhythm

During my twenties, there was one poet among my peers whom I wanted to knee-cap. That was John Newlove. When I read his 1965 collection Moving In Alone, *I discovered a batch of steely, laconic poems, like "In Libya":*

I was in libya,
with jason & there
wrote a poem of it, a bad one

being numbed by
all that death
& the death to come, young
to be slaughtered:

a bad way to write
poems, & I was in syracuse
when lamachos died & the army died

later & it was said, These,
having done what men could, suffered
what men must: & wrote a poem of it
& poems of all the deaths to come.

That stopped me cold. The poem was tight-lipped, but you could sense the outrage at the way soldiers are used and discarded — "young to be slaughtered." Plus, Newlove was doing something with line breaks that called for active retribution. Here was a writer my age, with lines so cleanly etched they probed the reflexes of my own work, exposing its mannered stiffness. How had he learned to write this way? And where could I get some myself?

This may seem like a curious lead-in to an essay on micro-rhythms. But they're what poems live by. And John was at home with the rhythms of free verse from early on, when I still had no clue. So I hope you'll indulge this mordant encomium.

I. Prosody

It starts with rhythm, that much I know. A poem lives and breathes by the way it moves — its pace and gait and proportions. It can unfold with the shapely aplomb of a gavotte, or lurch like a punched gut, or move with a quicksilver stutter and glide. Each rhythm shapes the flow with a distinctive logic, scans the world with a syntax of its own.

◆

Different rhythms kick in at different scales.

This essay is about micro-rhythms, which function at the level of syllables ... of single words ... of a line ... of several lines.

Meaning, this is about prosody.

◆

Why fixate on prosody?

Because it's the basis for everything else. You can't write a decent poem without a feel for longer rhythms. But without a feel for micro-rhythms — without a working prosody — you can't write a decent line. What do you have to steer by? If there's no rhythmic norm at the granular level, ten words on the page will just sit there — a random chunk of prose, with arbitrary line breaks.

Many things flow from prosody. Nothing precedes it.

◆

But right away there's a complication. In English-language poetry, there are currently two separate prosodies in use — two different models of micro-rhythmic coherence.

- One is metrical prosody. It goes back at least eight hundred years, to well before Chaucer's time. During most of that span, it was the only game in town.
- The second is free verse, which was devised one hundred years ago. It ditched one of the key elements in metrical prosody, and found a different way to make micro-rhythms work.

But the metrical model didn't curl up and die. It's still a living tradition, and poets today gravitate to whichever prosody feels like home.

◆

This isn't a detailed history of micro-rhythm. Nor is it a scholarly survey, with examples galore. It's a love letter — to both prosodies, radically different though they are. Stroking the ripple and clarion strut of sense on the page. Their body music.

II. Metrical Prosody

1.

Metrical prosody governed the micro-rhythms of English poetry for centuries. And it also governed the blank verse of Elizabethan and Jacobean plays, including Shakespeare's.

Its best known feature is *meter*. And for readers who came to loathe the subject in high school, I guarantee: this won't be a catalogue of trochaic tetrameters and dactylic hexameters. It's true, there are many different meters. But they all perform the same surprising function, and that's what we'll explore here.

Starting with the basics.

2.

What is a meter? The elements are simple enough:

- Every meter contains a certain number of beats — a beat being the rhythmic equivalent of a syllable.
- In each meter, the beats are organized in a specific rhythmic pattern.
- The pattern depends on the degree of stress or emphasis given to each beat.
- There are only two degrees of metrical stress: strong and weak. Heavy and light. Stressed and unstressed.
- The meter contains no words — just indicators for "strong" and "weak."
- As a first approximation: a meter is an abstract rhythmic model, which presents a particular pattern of stressed and unstressed beats. The whole meter corresponds to a single line of verse.

3.

Here's the most common meter in English poetry:

da - DUM | da - DUM | da - DUM | da - DUM | da - DUM

That string of das and DUMs is the meter called "iambic pentameter."

Like all meters, it's subdivided into identical units — called "feet." Here there are five feet, so the meter is pentameter ("penta" meaning "five" in Greek). And there are two beats in each foot, arranged in the pattern "da - DUM" — a weak beat followed by a strong one. This foot is called an "iamb"; hence the meter is iambic pentameter. We'll take it as our working example.

◆

The first "da - DUM" supplies the key to the whole thing. That initial iamb is repeated four times, to fill out the pentameter line. Then the whole meter is repeated in the second line ... in the third ... the fourth ... the fifth ... till the end of the poem. The meter can hurtle along, or it can go slowly, or even pause. But there will never be a variation in the pattern of stresses (unless the poet changes the meter). A given meter is fixed for as long as the poet is using it.

What we don't yet know is: what do poets use the meter for?

4.

Here's one common answer. It's often said that poets "follow the meter" when they write a poem. They reproduce its pattern of stresses — and that's where the rhythm comes from, at the micro-level.

This is almost 100% wrong. But it's wrong in a useful way, so let's give it a whirl. And since the meter applies to a single line, let's see what happens with one line from *Hamlet*: "To be, or not to be, that is the question."

What do we hear if we inflect the line according to the metrical pattern — the familiar "da-DUM | da-DUM | da-DUM | da-DUM |

da-DUM"? To hear the result properly, you have to speak the line out loud. It'll sound like this:

> To BE, | or NOT | to BE, | that IS | the QUES- (tion)

Let's cut Shakespeare some slack, and disregard the clumsy dangling "-tion" at the end. It's the fourth foot that goes seriously astray. Following the meter forces us to say, "that IS | the QUES-tion" — which is not how anybody who speaks English would inflect the words. We'd say, "THAT is | the QUES-tion." Unfortunately, the bard couldn't make the meter work here.

Notice that he could have fixed the problem with a simple change of wording. The improved version would read, "To BE, | or NOT | to BE — | is THAT | the QUES-tion?" Now the natural emphasis of the words ("is THAT") aligns with the stress-pattern of the meter ("da-DUM"). But Shakespeare failed to spot that solution.

◆

Maybe he was more adept when it came to poetry. Here's the opening line of Sonnet 116, pronounced as per the metrical pattern:

> Let ME | not TO | the MAR- | riage OF | true MINDS

But that's even worse; it turns the whole line into gobbledygook. What about a modern poet like Yeats? Here's the first line of "Sailing to Byzantium":

> That IS | no COUN- | try FOR | old MEN. | The YOUNG

Yikes! Each of these lines is in iambic pentameter — but following the stress-pattern of the meter produces gibberish. Were the poets so inept they couldn't make the words fit into the meter?

5.

The answer, of course, is that the words weren't *supposed* to fit into the meter. Or not all the time. In fact, that's almost the last thing they were supposed to do. A non-stop succession of "da-DUMs" would put a reader to sleep by the tenth line.

But if the actual, syllable-by-syllable rhythm — the sequence of light and heavy stresses we use when we read a poem — isn't dictated by the meter, what *is* it based on? And come to think of it: why set up a meter at all, if you're going to keep messing it up?

Something is going on that we haven't uncovered yet. Let's take a step back, and start over.

6.

In a metrical poem, a reader registers the stress-pattern of the meter in the first few lines — kinesthetically, not analytically or even consciously. And since the meter never changes, that regular rhythm will go on ticking in the reader's body-sense for the rest of the poem or play. It will be reinforced whenever the dominant foot — in this case, the iamb — gets an uninterrupted run. As it does in the first three feet of our sample line: "To BE, | or NOT | to BE, | ..."

Which is to say: the meter acts as a ground bass or drone throughout the poem.

7.

For reasons that will emerge shortly, it will be helpful to consider this ground-bass as an independent rhythmic system, which operates in the poem from beginning to end. I'll call it a *protocol.* Thus we can speak of "the metrical protocol," meaning the repetitive rhythmic pattern that underlies the entire work at the syllabic level.

8.

And this brings us to the point we've been missing. In metrical poetry, there are *two separate protocols* operating at the same time. One is the meter, and here the stress-pattern is fixed, regular, repetitive. The second is what I'll call the *spoken protocol*: the succession of light and heavy stresses that emerges when we speak the words in a natural way, as we would in conversation. In this spoken protocol, we *point* the text — emphasizing some syllables and words, soft-pedalling others — to convey particular shades of meaning and feeling. And in this second protocol, the stresses are irregular, spontaneous, alive.

◆

Consider the range of possible emphases that can occur in a single foot, within the spoken protocol. The strong accent can shift to a different position from the metrical placement. Three syllables can skip along in the space reserved for two. There may be no strong spoken stress at all, in a syllabic group where the meter makes us hear one. There may be only four strong stresses in a five-foot line. The spoken micro-rhythms are shifting and unpredictable.

9.

And therein lies the genius of metrical prosody. It plays two rhythmic protocols against each other, so the variable one dances in and out of phase with the fixed one.

This is called *syncopation*, and it's one of the deepest rhythmic pleasures there is. It consists of setting up expectations for the strong and weak beats, via the meter — and then breaking the pattern. So we experience both rhythms simultaneously: the one we expect, and the one we actually hear. For whatever reason, this syncopation gives great pleasure to human beings. And for centuries it provided the basic language of micro-rhythms in English poetry.

10.

Let's return to the line from *Hamlet*. And let's scan it the way it might actually be spoken by an actor. Here I'll use the symbols | and || and ||| to indicate pauses of differing lengths (which, you'll recall, don't alter the stress-pattern of the meter).

> To BE | or NOT | to BE: ||| THAT || is the QUES-(tion).

How does that spoken reading compare with the metrical pattern? The first three feet are regular iambs — stressed the same way as in the meter. But the fourth and fifth feet are syncopated. In this scansion, the fourth foot is a single strong beat ("THAT"), and the fifth is a three-beat foot ("is the QUES-"). Those miniscule deviations are counterpointed against the regular iambs that our bodies silently supply. And the beat goes on.

11.

Syncopation unfolds largely beneath the reader's threshold of awareness. Some of the spoken stresses coincide with the meter; others diverge from it. And maybe one spoken line in ten will reproduce the meter beat for beat. But provided the two protocols don't diverge for too long, the reader will continue to sense the meter ticking beneath the rhythmic freeplay of the spoken text — keeping the subliminal micro-rhythms carnal and vivacious. The more resourceful the poet, the more compelling the dance of the micro-rhythms. (Despite our earlier misreading of Shakespeare, he was a virtuoso at syncopation.)

12.

This is where discussions of metrical prosody often take a wrong turn. They could explore syncopation. But instead, they get bogged down in cataloguing all the possible meters. That's easy to talk about. But it leaves the real glory of metrical prosody — its syncopation — unaddressed, and perhaps inaudible to an apprentice reader.

13.

But this raises a fresh question. When it comes to the spoken protocol, what is the correct way to stress the non-metrical material? If the meter is the drone but not the actual guide, how do we know which syllables to emphasize when the writer syncopates?

Sometimes the answer is clear. In the line from *Hamlet*, for instance, the two words "that is" should clearly be inflected as "THAT is," not "that IS." No argument there.

But much of the time, there's no obvious answer. The reader, or the actor, could inflect the line in several different ways. It's a game of improvisation.

14.

And there are two stages of improv. The first is the poet/dramatist's. As they write, they riff against the repetitive meter — using whatever syllabic stresses achieve lift-off.

The second stage comes when the reader or actor enters the picture. They'll face a series of granular choices — which syllables to stress, which to de-emphasize. And many of those decisions will be based on the sheer pleasure of improvisation. What's neat is that there is often no single right option; there are several. Speaker's choice. Though some ways of syncopating the text will feel more attuned, and others less so.

15.

For an example, let's go back to *Hamlet*. Here are two possible readings of our sample line — first, the fairly conservative one we've already seen:

> To BE, | or NOT | to BE, ||| THAT || is the QUES-tion:

And here's a more radical reading — where there are only four strong beats in the line:

> To BE, | or NOT to be, ||| THAT || is the QUES-tion:

Is one reading right, and the other one wrong? Not at all. They give subtly different weightings to the words — and each is legitimate. Finally, all you can say is that some deep, intuitive delight in improvisation configures the micro-rhythms. Kinesthetic play. Body music.

16.

Since micro-rhythms in the metrical protocol are fixed, while in the spoken protocol they're variable, the capsule formula for metrical prosody is "fixed/variable."

What sense of coherence is manifest here? It's possible to discern signature moves in the prosody of individual poets, and these enact the syntax of order that each poet intuits. But going further: how is coherence parsed in metrical prosody at large? What underlying scansion of the world does "fixed/variable" embody?

It says: there is a fixed order. And at the same time, there is a spontaneous flux. Truth in rhythm consists of orchestrating order and flux at the same time. Without meter, measure, degree, the freeplay of particulars would degenerate into chaos. And without unscheduled play, the structure would become an iron grid. It is within this intuition — of local freedom overlapping with established order — that rhythmic meaning emerges in metrical poetry.

17.

Now, let's take a giant leap.

For centuries, this double audition governed the micro-rhythms of poetry. And in broad terms, it seems to me, that resonated with the sense of the world's coherence which obtained in Europe during its ascendancy. There was a fixed natural law, established by God, as well as a fixed social hierarchy, established by tradition and brute force. But simultaneous with these rigid constraints, people and things were sometimes free to move spontaneously, unpredictably.

That is, it was inherent in the very nature of things to be rigorously ordered and freely variable at the same time. Those were the twin categories within which the world went about cohering, making sense.

Which is to say: prosody rhymed with cosmology. The microcosm and the macrocosm were of a piece.

III. Free Verse

18.

THOSE WERE GLORY YEARS FOR POETRY. GLORY CENTURIES. But by 1850 or so, metrical prosody was no longer a fit for some English-speaking poets. For whatever reason, meter was starting to lose its universal currency.

Some poets experimented with non-metrical alternatives; of these, the most robust were Whitman's dithyrambic line and Hopkins' sprung rhythm. But Hopkins was inimitable. And while a number of poets would absorb Whitman's rhythms, most of them struggled to find a voice of their own when they did.

If we freeze the frame shortly after 1900, then, we see this picture. It was still possible for major poets to work in meter — as Yeats was doing, as Stevens would later do, and as many lesser poets would keep on doing. But for the poets who were no longer at home with metrical rhythm, there was no shared prosody that let them move naturally on the page.

19.

This created a practical impasse. Consider:

- Without meter as the ground bass, how do you handle the spoken rhythms in a poem? You can't syncopate them — there's nothing to syncopate them against. Is there any music left that's specific to poetry? Aren't you just writing prose, chopped up into random lines?
- And what is a line, if there's no meter? Where should you divide a string of words, when there's no longer a pre-set line length?
- Less urgently: what about the left-hand margin — what anchors it now? Why should a line start at the left side of the page? Why should it start in any specific position?

The more deeply you enter post-metrical listening, the blurrier things get. The prosody has become impossibly fluid. Without meter to keep things stable, what is the basis of rhythmic coherence — any basis? any coherence?

20.

The breakthrough came with the discovery of free verse. The term has a varied history, but I take it to mean poetry written in a new prosody, which Ezra Pound started exploring in 1912.

That sets off an alarm, however. In matters of pure technique, Pound was a genius. His innovations would change the course of English poetry. But outside the technical realm, he became increasingly erratic: a megalomaniac, a rabid antisemite, and during World War II a cheerleader for Hitler's ally Mussolini. So we have to ask: was Pound's new prosody coloured by his gimcrack theories and toxic beliefs?

As far as I can judge, the answer is no. Pound pioneered free verse in his twenties, when he was still of relatively clear mind. And more basically: there is no necessary connection between the new prosody and any specific belief.

That has been the de facto conclusion of history as well. Free verse quickly became the non-metrical prosody of choice in the English-speaking world, and poets of many persuasions have been using it for more than a century.

The challenge is to decipher how it works; what follows is one man's take.

21.

Quick summary: Pound solved the post-metrical dilemma by tackling an entirely different issue. When he succeeded with that, the loss of meter and syncopation ceased to matter.

22.

Consider a passage from Pound's long poem *The Cantos* (selected, almost at random, from Canto 82). The passage concerns the long, slow struggle to bring "the news" to an obtuse civilization. It's not clear what the news consists of. But — as often with Pound — it's not the content of the passage that's compelling; it's the music.

> … and the news is a long time moving
> a long time in arriving
> thru the impenetrable
> crystalline, indestructible
> ignorance of locality.
> The news was quicker in Troy's time
> a match on Cnidos, a glow worm on Mitylene …

Let's ease past the cryptic references and abstract concepts, and focus on the way the passage moves on the page. It unfolds with undeniable rhythmic power. But where does that power come from? More specifically: what is Pound doing with the micro-rhythms?

23.

The key is in the pointing.

A stage director *points* the flow of a scene. A violinist *points* a passage in a sonata. That is, they etch the rhythms cleanly, coax out the inner dynamics. They guide our rhythms of attention, so we absorb *this* phrase, *this* pool of feeling, and glide past others. Without such pointing, the performance will be muddy, lumpy, lacking in focus.

What Pound devised was a new, non-metrical way to point the micro-rhythms of a poem.

24.

How does the pointing work?

Like metrical prosody, free verse relies on two protocols. Two rhythmic systems, neither of which is metrical. Each protocol has its own techniques for pointing, and Pound discovered how to play the pointing of one against the pointing of the other — creating a flexible new language for micro-rhythms.

25.

And what are the two protocols?

- The first is *syntax*, as found in everyday speech and writing.
- The second is what I'll call *notation*. It relies on line breaks and margins.
- Both protocols are variable. That is, the poet has to improvise the rhythm in both systems — and do so simultaneously.
- Free prosody operates on a larger scale than metrical prosody does. We have to track it across two or more lines, rather than within a single line.

26.

Let's look at the familiar system first.

We know what we mean by syntax: the arrangement of grammatical units in a sentence. The way subject, verb and object configure what's being said; the way phrases and subordinate clauses are massed and counterposed. The syntax points the meaning of a sentence with a specific kinetic logic.

And we can expand the term, to include the way consecutive sentences are marshalled. That creates a further range of pointing. Two quick sentences, leading to a mighty periodic surge. Staccato question: staccato reply. If the writer is savvy, the syntax will guide us through a coherent journey of attending.

27.

Now consider the syntax of the excerpt from *The Cantos*. It builds on a series of parallel phrases. Here's the first pair, presented in the opening lines:

> ... and the news is a long time moving
> a long time in arriving

The second pair follows immediately. Once again the phrases are parallel, but now they're spread over three lines, with a more complex layout.

> thru the impenetrable
> crystalline, indestructible
> ignorance of locality.

And the third pair of phrases occupies a single line at the end:

> a match on Cnidos, a glow worm on Mitylene ...

What is the cumulative effect? The repetition of parallel phrases points the content with a deliberate, measured rhythm, reinforcing the gravitas of the content itself. There's even a suggestion of call-and-response within each pair ("a long time moving / a long time in arriving"). At the same time (to jump ahead briefly), the three different ways in which the pairs are laid out keeps the structure from becoming formulaic. Pound has achieved a potent music by means of the syntax.

But while that shows a mastery of syntactic rhythm, it hardly qualifies as a radical departure. It's when he combines free syntax with free notation that Pound breaks new ground.

28.

What does "free notation" involve? There are two main elements: line breaks, and margins. We'll start with line breaks, and the way they govern the pace.

Suppose you break the line after a period; that creates a pause in the forward momentum. Break it after an adjective, however, and the reader is yanked ahead to complete the meaning. Using that technique, the pace of a poem can be speeded up or slowed down from line to line.

With variable line breaks, you can also swing between long lines and short ones, to echo the rhythms of the syntax or depart from them. The options are legion, and many free-verse poets notate exclusively with line breaks.

29.

If they go further, the second element in free notation is the margins. Which lines to indent? How far? This is visual and spatial rhythm, and we register it first with the eye and the body. Which makes it harder to pinpoint the rhythmic effects analytically.

Let's try another approach. Here's the full passage again, for ease of reference:

> ... and the news is a long time moving
> a long time in arriving
> thru the impenetrable
> crystalline, indestructible
> ignorance of locality.
> The news was quicker in Troy's time
> a match on Cnidos, a glow worm on Mitylene ...

Now let's change the notation to the traditional format — with no indents:

> ... and the news is a long time moving
> a long time in arriving
> thru the impenetrable
> crystalline, indestructible
> ignorance of locality.
> The news was quicker in Troy's time
> a match on Cnidos, a glow worm on Mitylene ...

The difference between the two versions is palpable. To overstate slightly: the first layout dances; the second one plods along. The format with the staggered margins gives us something the flush-left format can't. We'll return to this shortly.

30.

How do the two protocols interact? To get some idea, listen to how Pound uses them to tell an unlikely little story.

At first, the notation reinforces the syntax. In the opening lines, the break comes between "a long time moving" and "a long time in arriving" — that is, at the obvious pause point. But in the second pair of phrases, the notation is more challenging. Each break comes between an adjective and its noun, and the little kick of unpredictability (what will "impenetrable" modify? what about "indestructible"?) jostles the composure of the pronouncement. How will the rhythm respond to this disturbance? The third pair of phrases is set as a single, stable line: "a match on Cnidos, a glow worm in Mitylene." Which imparts a sense of equipoise, of rhythmic completion.

A whole miniature story has been told in the shifting rhythms. A story of rhythm itself.

31.

And a final example of Pound's musical chops. As he brings the passage to a close, he makes a startling swerve: he shifts into the conventions of metrical verse.

> The news was quicker in Troy's time
> a match on Cnidos, a glow worm in Mitylene ...

These lines abandon indents, and hew to the flush-left margin. And — even more unexpectedly — the final line is in iambic pentameter. We can sense the five-beat meter beneath the spoken words. That burnishes and deepens the feeling of rhythmic completion.

32.

Now let's go back to the staggered margins. They set up an additional level of pointing, creating parallel or off-centre relations among the lines. And in a subtle way, they extend and redefine the space in which a poem exists.

Read the passage again. Perhaps you can sense how the placement of lines is choreographed by a shifting field of energy. It's as if the white space in which the words are embedded has become part of the poem, shaping the layout with spatial and visual rhythms. This gives the words a further dimension to breathe in, along with the verbal one. It's what Charles Olson called "composition by field," and it amplifies the very nature of coherence in a poem.

33.

So the syntax and the notation work in tandem — creating a rhythmic movement which is almost liturgical, yet still locally quirky. No other poem will repeat this particular scoring; each move in free prosody is a one-off improvisation. It's hard to do well. But the craft of free verse is wonderfully flexible; it allows a poet room to orchestrate micro-rhythms in the key of whatever. Which gives poets of many different kinds a rhythmic language to work in.

34.

We can now ask: what generates the particular music of a free poem?

That's like asking what generates the variable stresses in a metrical poem. In a way, both are instigated by the content. But that's just the point of departure. The poet is goosed along by an intuitive *something* — by the rhythmic dance that's itching to happen, if he can get the notation talking to the syntax the way they're straining to. What generates the music is the open-ended tug and telos of improvisation. No recipes; no nets.

Finally, it is generated by the poet's intuition of coherence. By the tumble and play of what-is. The body music of world.

35.

It fell to Pound to discover this new prosody. And that expanded the way poetry can be written. But making a discovery of this magnitude wasn't unique to Ezra Pound. At around the same time, a handful of scientists and artists were re-imagining the grammar of coherence in their own fields. They weren't just applying the received model of order to unfamiliar subject matter; they were calling the model itself into question. Mulching the paradigms; sussing out new ones. The version of coherence that had ruled their discipline for centuries no longer fitted the way things are.

Thus Einstein in physics, then Heisenberg. Thus Schoenberg

in music. Thus — decades earlier — Lobachevsky and Riemann in geometry. Thus Picasso; thus Proust and Joyce. When Pound discovered free prosody, he was on the same mission as these other titans. Each acting independently, with little or no awareness that a similar quest was playing out in neighbouring domains.

Some inscrutable necessity was surfacing across the board.

36.

This brings us to the primary question: how is order parsed in free prosody? Beyond the signature moves of individual poets, what scansion of the world does it embody?

What's new in free prosody is that there is no fixed frame of reference. Unlike in metrical prosody, both its protocols are variable. Thus the capsule formula for free verse is "variable/variable."

Free prosody says, the poem and the world may cohere — but there is no privileged, changeless framework providing that coherence. Rather, meaningful order emerges in the interplay of relative systems. And we register it intuitively, in a spirit of improvisation. So the act of making sense of the world helps to determine the sense we make of it. In ways that are difficult to comprehend, we ourselves participate in the coming-to-be of meaningful order. Yet at the same time, some of our improvisations ring true, and others don't. We can't just make stuff up. The search for what is the case, in prosody as in cosmology, is both a free and a rigorous discipline.

37.

And a personal recollection. When I was young, several lifetimes ago, I wrote my master's thesis on *The Cantos*. But not on its prosody. I was intrigued by Pound's innovations in large-scale structure, and I planned to compare the *Cantos* with the general theory of relativity. (Not being a mathematician, I worked from Einstein's guide for lay readers, *Relativity: The Special and General Theory*.) Could you map Pound's revolutionary hunches about coherence in poetry against Einstein's recasting of the basic categories of physics? At some deep level, did their formal intuitions coincide? Or was the whole thing a fever dream of my own? I wanted to test the conjecture.

It was a big ask for a master's thesis, and in the end I limited the enquiry to Pound's structural innovations. And shortly thereafter, I bailed. I left the academy, and swapped intellectual reasoning for poetic sniffing-about. So I never pursued the conjecture — at least, not in the analytic terms I assumed were the only legitimate form of thought.

But that was years ago, when I was young.

Re-Greening the Undermusic

For a number of years, the Ralph Gustafson Lecture was presented at Vancouver Island University. Each year a poet was asked to read from their work and talk about their poetics. I got the call in 2012.

It was a chance to take stock of fifty years of writing. And in the first half of the lecture, I covered some of the ground I've explored in these essays. In the second half, by contrast, I had to scramble to catch up with a dramatic swerve my work had taken latterly.

And where do things go from here? How will writing square with aging? ... That's something a recent poem wrestles with. You'll find it in the Coda.

ONE THING I ADMIRE ABOUT THE GUSTAFSON LECTURE SERIES is its down-to-earth approach. "Read some of your poems; discuss your poetics." That's the remit. I don't know any other literary forum that gets down to the nitty-gritty so directly.

Mind you, inviting a poet to talk about craft can be misleading. It can suggest that you start with a batch of portable techniques, and simply apply them to whatever subject comes along. But in my case, at least, that's not how it works. Most of the time I'm groping in the dark, trying to cobble a few words together that feel right. Sometimes the words begin to hum with a kind of music I hadn't expected, so I follow wherever that leads. And eventually, if I'm lucky, it may turn into a real poem, or sequence, or even a whole book. And it's only then that I can grasp analytically what I was doing intuitively before. So the poetry comes first, and it proceeds by trial and error; the conscious poetics emerge later. They're a rear-view mirror, not a GPS guide.

Now take it a step further. If you survey my work from the last five decades, you'll see many changes in technique. But when you look at the whole span, are these technical developments just a series of unrelated moves? Or is there a larger or deeper pattern? That's the question I want to explore here.

◆

When I started writing, in the early 1960s, I found myself in a dilemma. I loved the great tradition of British poetry, from Chaucer to Yeats — I'd been thoroughly immersed in it during my undergraduate years. And the poems I wrote were dutiful attempts to follow in that lineage. Unfortunately, they were lousy poems. My own imagination wasn't at home there; quite apart from my limitations as an apprentice poet, I was trying to enter a tradition I didn't belong in, like a runner who keeps training for the high jump. I had a dim sense of a different music beckoning — a different way of hearing words on the page. But I had no idea what it would sound like, so nothing I wrote was tuned to this unknown wavelength.

How did I resolve the dilemma? I didn't. For seven years I kept banging my head against the wall, trying to write the way I thought I should. Eventually I produced a book of sonnet variations, *Kingdom of Absence*. Here's an example:

Not sample handfuls of the world's galore,
nor rich and manic triumphs in my craft,
nor peace, nor sex, nor power, nor the nod
of those few men I honour in this wrack,
nor supercharging of the senses, nor
the inwarding of world, and not the climb
and kindling of the spirit, where it lifts
and flowers, standing gently into Being,
but this: in the blank heartlands of absence —
my house, my street, my foolish life — in these
deserted reaches of the living void
may I, like some before me, find the way
by waiting, lost, dispersed, to come to be
sufficient to the measure of abyss.

That may not be the worst poem ever written, but it's hardly a roaring success. It's knee-deep in abstractions. And since we're focusing on craft, let me single out the rhythm. It's iambic pentameter, but there's no subtlety or bite in the way the meter is handled. And on a larger scale, the content has been shoehorned into one of the standard sonnet structures: a quatrain, another quatrain, and a six-line conclusion. But there's no sense that this is a natural fit for the poet. He's simply following an abstract pattern, reproducing it from the outside. In fact he's spinning his wheels, going nowhere.

◆

Kingdom of Absence came out in the spring of 1967. And with that, the dam broke. I sat up scribbling night after night all that summer, and what came through was a real voice. Somehow I had tapped into a live energy source, and it erupted in long, tumbling lines that eddied and lunged.

Here's how it opens. The speaker is sitting in front of Toronto's New City Hall, breathing polluted air, and sensing spectral human shapes in the smog:

> Often I sit in the sun and brooding over the city, always
> in airborne shapes among the pollution I hear them, returning;
> pouring across the square
> in fetid descent they darken the towers
> and the wind-swept place of meeting, and whenever
> the thick air clogs my breathing it teems with their presence.
> Many were born in Canada, and living unlived lives they died
> of course but died truncated, stunted, never at
> home in native space and not yet
> citizens of a human body of kind. And it is Canada
> that specialized in this deprivation. Therefore the spectres arrive,
>   congregating
> in bitter droves, thick in the April sunlight,
> accusing us and we are no different, though you would not expect
> the furies assembled in hogtown and ring me round, invisible, demanding
> what time of our lives we wait for till we shall come to be. …

The poem was *Civil Elegies*, and it arrived in a torrent; the entire book-length sequence was written and published within a year.

What had happened? I'd realized that my natural medium was not the sonnet, but a looser meditative form. And for a meditation to find its path, it has to be roomy in length, and open in structure. And more basically, I was connecting with the teeming rhythmic energy I'd been tantalized by for so long. If I just sat and waited, I could sense a swoop and pummel and glide, a simultaneous *whoosh* and throb — many vibrations at once. I felt them humming in my body, even though there was no physical source. What was it? I had no idea. Where did it come from? I couldn't say. But the kinesthetic pulsation was unmistakable, and it could govern the way a poem moved. It furnished a kind of undermusic, which the poem sought to track and embody.

I had no theory to explain this rhythmic cascade. But I did give it a name; for lack of a better term, I called it *cadence*. And I conjectured that I'd become open to cadence when I relinquished the colonial ways of framing experience that I'd inherited, and listened to my own here-and-now. But as for what cadence consisted of, or where it came from, I had no idea.

In any case, I found an unexpected energy muscling into words. And on the technical front, its pressure showed up first in the structure of sentences. In the syntax, which guides the reader's attention. Now the syntax was getting yanked and propelled all over the place. A sentence might start in one direction, but then it would swerve to include another urgent something, and then another. There was a say-everything-at-once quality to this pulsing energy, and at times it stretched conventional syntax almost to the breaking point. For an example, look at the final sentence in the passage above, starting "Therefore the spectres arrive ..."

◆

The 1968 version of *Civil Elegies* had all it could handle to keep up with this teeming undermusic. But in the next few years, I started to chafe. The voice of the elegies was public and stentorian, and that felt right for the subject: what it means to be a citizen of Canada. But the declamatory voice had become restrictive, drowning out other potential wavelengths, other kinds of music. And I'd begun to sense a more private, more musing tonality wanting to enter: a seeker's voice. So I went back and revised the sequence — and that marked the next stage in my poetics. I wrote two new elegies, and tinkered some of the others, to incorporate the quieter voice. It could sound like this:

> Master and Lord, where
> are you?
> A man moves back and forth
> between what must be done to save the world
> and what will save his soul,

> and neither is real. For many years
> I could not speak your name, nor now but
> even stilled at times by openings like
> joy my whole life
> aches, the streets I walk along to work declare
> your absence, the headlines
> declare it, the nation, and
> over and over the harried lives I
> watch and live with, holding my breath and
> sometimes a thing rings true —
> they all give way and declare your real absence. ...

Here the lines are shorter, more sinuous, and the splaying of the syntax is less extreme. There's a certain balance in the way things come at us: "A man moves back and forth / between what must be done to save the world / and what will save his soul, / and neither is real." That allows for a calmer meditative progress, even if the subject itself is far from calm.

◆

This brings us to 1972, when the revised version of the *Elegies* appeared. I had discovered that cadence could shape the way a poem moved. And I'd gone a step further, recognizing that a poem didn't have to be in a single voice. You could counterpoint two different tonalities, and their interplay would create a sonic narrative of its own.

Over the next 25 years, I extended this approach in several directions. The first took the handling of voice a step further. If you could have two voices in a poem — say, a declamatory public tone, and a musing private one — why not broaden that vocal range? What if there were three distinct tonalities? Or what if you kept shifting through a whole panoply of voices, so that at one moment the poem was chatty, at the next grave and liturgical, then sweetly lyrical, then coarse and vituperative? What if the poem allowed as many vocal strains onto the page as possible? I latched onto the term *polyphony* — "many voices" — for what I was doing.

By way of example, consider four pieces from a sequence called *Riffs*, which tells the story of a love affair. The woman has gone away, and the speaker is trying to preserve their high-voltage loving, if only in memory. What I invite you to tune into here is the wide range of voices he speaks in, as he lingers over different facets of their affair:

19

Wal, acey deucey
    trey divide —
I'm a guy
    with a fine wide-eyed

lady freckles too &
    squirms when she
feels good I feel so
    good just

doin aw
    shucks
tricks an she's
    SOFISTIKATED!

18

    Eerie
articulations of

    love-
space:

    delicate
angles:

arousal.

Will I
    trace this

deft a
    space upon your
body?

Would you be
                here?

31

    The angels'
cure for when they miss someone *very* bad is
    malt whiskey.

    'Dja
know that?
    I never knew that.

    Found out
my own way, special,
    just since you

    went away and to-
night at 2:48 a.m. I am
    practising up being an angel twinkle twinkle mud

39

Pen-
ultimate lady, alive — sweet

skin and sesame:
why do we ever rub con-

tours, if not to conjure
shapes of what we aren't and

crave to be? ...
Touching you I am

meat & pronto, I lounge in the chutzpah of
flesh; then woozy with

laughter and midnight and
caring, pure

carnal
panache — you, you, you in your frabjous parade —

how should I
reach for more?

Yet always behind you (this is
why I shy away), barely be-

yond you
is

nothing at all ...
Lady,

do not be offended when I
go there.

And on and on it goes, flashing through a whole kaleidoscope of voices. Which enacts the sense of a larger life — and an ampler, richer world — that arises when you fall in love, and careen from goofy to gobstruck to grave.

◆

But there's a technical challenge in polyphonic poetry. Namely: how do you get from one voice to the next? As far as I can see, there are only two options: a sudden *jump-cut*, or a more gradual *segue*.

In *Riffs*, the transitions were almost all jump-cuts. Each poem has its own distinct timbre, so the shifts of voice, from one piece to the next, come abruptly. But you can also morph through a transition more gradually. Take this example, from a later sequence called "Nightwatch." The speaker's marriage has broken up, and at first he had blamed the dissolution on the vogue for existentialism, which holds that we're free to reinvent our lives at will. But now he recoils from that grandiose alibi — and as he does, the voice goes through a series of gradual shifts, sliding from sarcasm to plain speech to grave self-accusation. It's this incremental bending of tone — in contrast to abrupt jump-cuts — that I invite you to follow.

> But who am I trying to kid?
> "Modernity Wrecked My Marriage" —
>   that'll wow them in Reno.
> "Divorce Case Shock: Nietzsche Named as Third Party" —
>   there's a bleat with legs!
> But what right did I have to be married?
> It comes to that.
>   For I, who am not a vicious man, was barely here
>   for the ones I love.
>   I lived in another country: my mind, or
>   where my mind kept going —
>   where something thrummed, and
>   myself was almost the music;
> and the truer that place, the worse my dereliction.
>   But the children paid the price.
> Their cause-besotted father gave them
> nothing to live by, and I see my darlings reaching out for sustenance
> in the city of kicks and neon, who can neither respect me nor
> suffer me to hold them, for they know
> the botch I have made of my time ...

Mind you, when I was sussing out a poem's polyphony I wasn't worrying about jump-cuts or segues. I was just trying to make the thing *sound* right, *feel* right. There might be transitions of both kinds in the space of a few lines. And at some points, I'd be hard put to specify the precise difference in tone between one little run and the next. So I didn't start with a set of distinct vocal categories, and write to order. I followed my ear. Perhaps you can glimpse what a sumptuous field it was to play in — coaxing the jambalaya of voices the world gives off into a polyphonic journey on the page.

◆

The second discovery I made, along with "multiple voices," involved a poem's *layout.* As I tried to replicate the supple torrent of cadence, I realized that poems could be laid out much more fluidly on the page than the *Elegies* were. I was hardly the first person to make this discovery; I was building on the innovations of a flock of poets, from Ezra Pound on. But I developed my own conventions for choreographing the dance of words by means of the format.

Here's an example, from a poem called "The Gods." I was trying to imagine how, in times past, people experienced the natural world as a place of numinous power, the home of "gods." That's hard to fathom today, when we've developed such a convincing model of the world as value-free that we may not think of it as intrinsically awesome.

But I wasn't pursuing a philosophical argument. I was trying to imagine the older experience, of being brought to your knees by a power beyond yourself — in this case, by the sudden appearance of a bear. And I didn't want to describe the experience from the outside; I wanted to tattoo it, first-hand, on our nerve-ends as we read. The poem had to enact a staccato barrage of perceptions, each being barely processed before the next one hit. The awe-inspiring advent of the creature, and the welter of responses it triggers, had to overlap, feel jagged, disorienting.

Here's the layout I found when I tried to make that happen on the page:

And yet —
in the middle of one more day, in a clearing maybe sheer
godforce
calm on the lope of its pads
furred hot-breathing erect, at ease, catastrophic
harsh waves of stink, the
dense air clogged with its roaring and
ripples of power fork through us:
hair gone electric quick
pricklish glissando, the
skin mind skidding, balking is
HAIL
and it rears foursquare and we are jerked and owned and
forgive us and
brought to a welter, old
force & destroyer and
do not destroy us!
or if it seems good,
destroy us. ...

◆

In this open scoring, the most conspicuous feature is the staggered margins — the changing indents. The flush-left margin is no longer the recurring visual anchor; a new line can start anywhere. Once you take hold of that freedom, the poem can dance its way down the page with a swivel and glide that would be hard to bring off in the older, fixed-left-margin format.

Mind you, such freedom is disorienting — for the poet, first of all. If a new line can start anywhere on the page, how do you know where it *should* start? I wrestled with that, and eventually I devised a convention of my own. I set up a series of margins, so I'd have a structure to improvise against. In this passage (a fairly complex example), there are nine margins, each indented the same distance to the right of its predecessor. I used four taps on the space bar for each successive indent. So every line starts at one or another of the pre-set margins. And with that invisible grid as the framework, I orchestrated the poem's movement — feeling out a layout, by trial and error, that would choreograph what was being said in the most potent way. I wanted the pauses and spurts, and the quicker or longer return times, to enact the volatile rhythms of the content, as the great creature appears.

I'm giving you a glimpse behind the scenes here, a snapshot from a poet's workshop. Here's another glimpse. I'd learned from reading Al Purdy that *where* you break a line affects the pacing. If you break after a word like "but" or "the," it tugs the reader ahead. Whereas if you break after a period or comma, or simply after a discrete unit of meaning, the reader will pause for an extra millisecond before continuing. I learned how to move back and forth between those two kinds of line break, so the pace of forward movement would stay varied and fresh.

◆

I was always bothered by the question, How do you convey the nuances of open scoring when you read a poem out loud to an audience? And I've never found a satisfactory answer. You could try pausing for different lengths of time at the line breaks, to indicate something about the successive indents. Or you could give finger signals of some kind. But those are mechanical solutions, which would simply distract a listener. And I've concluded that poetry of this kind is finally rooted in the page. It exists simultaneously in the visual (reading) and the sonic (hearing) dimensions. But to experience its music fully, you have to *hear it out loud on the page.*

That said, a live reading has resources for which the page would give its eye teeth: changes in volume, in speed, even in body English. So it's a trade-off. But the subtle rhythms of visual scoring are essentially not communicable when you read a poem aloud.

◆

In 1996 I published a New and Selected, *Nightwatch*, which unwittingly brought this stage of my poetics to a close. For twenty-nine years I'd been tracking cadence in the ways I've described: orchestrating polyphonic voices, and pursuing an open layout on the page. It seemed like a field without limits.

But in the year 2000, something unexpected happened. I'd wanted for some time to address the dire state of the environment, and I started a long poem which was eloquent on the subject. But pretty soon I got restless. I felt as if I was composing an op-ed column; the poem was worthy, and earnest, and it bored the pants off me.

So I pitched the whole thing, and simply listened. And what came through was unlike anything I'd written before. It spooked me, to tell the truth. Because a poem could sound like this:

> Scribblescript portents unfold, world-
> to, worldfro.
> And to comb the signs, to
> stammer the uterine painscape
> in pidgin apocalypse — how now not
> gag on the unward, the once-upon, us-
> proud planet?

Or this:

> In wreck, in dearth, in necksong,
> godnexus gone to fat of the land,
> into the wordy desyllabification of evil — small
> crawlspace for plegics, 4, 3, 2, 1, un.

Or this — where "nothing" turns out to be the present participle of the unexpected verb "to noth":

And are creatures of
nothing.
I noth you noth we
long have we nothed we
shall noth, staunch in true
nothing we
noth in extremis, noth until
habitat heartstead green galore & species
relinquish the terrene ghosthold;
crumble to alphadud; stutter to rumours of *ing*.

What was going on? Were these even poems? They seemed more like dense *objects*, made out of — what *were* they made of? Words, obviously, but words with only a fitful resemblance to English. There was some new relation to language here. I'd been reading Paul Celan, a poet whose diction is often fractured, and that had opened the door. But now I was trying to follow wherever words led — and they were taking me to strange places, where the craft I'd developed for decades no longer applied.

But though I was flustered, I stayed with this new music. Here are three more of the whatchamacallits that surfaced over the next couple of years. In each case, I began with no idea what would emerge, from one word to the next.

In cess, in dis-
ownmost, in ripture,
in slo-mo history cease,
in bio in haemo in necro — yet how
dumbfound how
dazzled, how
mortally lucky to be.

Lullabye wept as
asia buckled,
rockabye einstein and all.

One for indigenous,
two for goodbye,
adam and eve and dodo.

Fly away mecca,
fly away rome,
lullabye wept in the lonely.

Once the iguanodon,
once the U.N.,
hush little orbiting gone.

With a *yes*, with a *no*, with a
yesno;
sonics in simuljam.

To habitate crossbeing.
To ride both reals at once. To least-
wise stay
vif in detritus/un-
lulled by the blessingbait green.

Gradually I began to get the hang of this bizarre wordscape. Language was no longer situated at a safe remove from the planetary crisis — able to hold it at arm's length, issuing objective pronouncements *about* it. The crisis had invaded language itself; words were already part of the global disaster. Which meant that, to give true testimony, they had to accept the very disintegration they were trying to articulate.

And once I twigged to that, something else clicked into place. In *Civil Elegies*, the undermusic of cadence had reshaped sentences — shanghaiing the syntax, splaying it around. What was happening here was an extension of that process. Only now the raw energy was erupting at a more elemental level still: in individual words. Demolishing some, remaking others, mashing syllables together. I was still hanging on for dear life to the energy of cadence, but now it was melting down my home medium, words themselves. The poems had become events in the larger conflict: tiny skirmishes, live scenes from the battlefront.

◆

I've spent most of the last decade catching up with this linguistic red alert. It led to a book called *Un,* then to a successor, *Yesno,* and finally to *Testament,* which unites the two books and recasts them. *Testament* has some new poems as well, and to my surprise they started to loosen up. They were longer, less crabbed, more accessible. I positioned them as periodic landmarks or beacons:

> Last call for a trashable planet,
> bring it on home.
> Bring it on *sotto,* bring it on
> shockabye. Bring it on oil-
> wise, soilwise, waterwise, methuselah —
> memory holes in the phyla, and
> bring it on home.
>
> (If home still
> has a home. If roots
> still grope for rootedness. If
> butcherama,
> botcherama, wide-screen
> world has not yet
> metamulched what is.)
>
> And farfew the habitat heroes,
> bring it on AWOL.
> Bring it on oilwork, soilwork, patchwork, be-
> gin again — through
> plagues of our fathers, blue
> *culpa.* And
> bring it on, bring it on home.

◆

We started with the stilted, conventional verse of *Kingdom of Absence*. From there, we tracked my route — through the onset of cadence, to polyphony and open scoring. And we've arrived at the pitted, seething wordscape of *Testament*. Let me return now to my original question: if there's a deeper coherence in this trajectory, what does it consist of?

Since I don't have a ready answer, I'll start with a series of probes, often in shorthand.

◆

First: what should we make of "cadence"? I've come to believe it's the active coherence of what-is, transmitted as a rich, untamed array of kinesthetic frequencies. It mediates the energy of things being themselves — of their being-at-all.

When a poet tunes in to cadence, *it* furnishes the undermusic of what he writes, the rhythmic lead. The reader may not experience the tumble of cadence directly, but he can track its spoor in the poem's shifting gait and timbre, and its volatile textures.

Or, starting from the other side: the poem is a kind of tuning fork or lightning rod for cadence. Its rhythmic trajectory enacts one account of the dynamics of being, the logos of cosmos. Provisional and patchy though the account may be.

This way of mapping the order of things differs from that of standard Western thinking. It doesn't wrangle their coherence into scrutability by organizing them according to abstract mental categories. Rather, it epitomizes their kinetic gestalts in the concrete rhythms of poetry.

◆

Secondly: what is the place of "nature" in a poem today?

It doesn't just serve as subject matter. The primary, full-tilt encounter with wilderness takes place right on the page — in the material dimension of words, and the undermusic that configures them. Whether or not the natural world is present as content, its energy of being — its torque and galumph and shimmy — is tuned to the matrix that sustains and inflects the words. So there is no absolute need to write about sunsets or whales, though there's no reason not to. If a poem is attuned, it's already fuelled by the force that makes a whale a whale, a sunset a sunset, a city street a city street.

And giving that energy its head, from one line to the next, is a deeper way of honouring and hewing to it than merely including a roll call of flora and fauna. If the dance of being inflects the dance of words, you're already immersed in the wild. That untrammeled energy has been blocked, violated, re-engineered by our civilization. But it's still present, in whatever beleaguered forms it has mutated into, and it can still configure the music of a poem.

◆

The poems I selected for *Nightwatch* were written between 1967 and 1996 (starting with *Civil Elegies*), and they sought to enact a polyphasic richness of being. *Testament* responds to a newer, more cataclysmic music. Its busted rhythms and collapsed, creation-gumbo language bespeak a phase change in the history of what-is.

◆

Think of Pollock or Rothko. The discovery that *paint* — paint alone; live gestures in colour and shape — can be the venue in which the world articulates itself.

But the parallel is only partial, since language isn't paint. Words have literal meanings, which they can never shed. Paint doesn't. So poetry is a hybrid, a mongrel. It has to both mean *and* be, represent *and* present.

◆

If we're going to survive, we have to re-green the planet. Or rather, we have to undo the catastrophic damage we've committed, so the earth can (possibly) re-green itself.

But what part does poetry play in that? I want to be as unsentimental as possible in asking the question.

◆

The real heavy lifting has to come from politicians, CEOs, activist leaders. The rest of us can vote thoughtfully, contribute to worthy causes, try to live in environmentally responsible ways. But our individual actions count for little; it's only if they're multiplied by many millions that they'll have an effect. And in the project of global re-greening, a poet has the same microscopic leverage as any other citizen. Poetry can't change the world.

◆

But there's more to it than that. A poet's home turf is words. And if the planet is re-greenable, language is one of the many domains where that needs to happen.

For words are imprinted with the titanic project of our civilization, which by its triumph is making the earth uninhabitable. And if I crave a transformation of the way humans dwell on earth, I have to look for the energies of transformation in my own small chunk of the territory. Otherwise, what right do I have to yap about criminally evasive politicians and corporate predators? Their task is nearly impossible too. The job of giving witness in words can't set the bar any lower than the much vaster job, of changing our imprint on earth.

Not as a substitute for concerted public action. But as one subsidiary arena of the challenge.

◆

So the question is not, What themes should a contemporary poet address? It's rather, What undermusic rings true? If the constitution of what-is undergoes a seismic change, events in words must change their rhythmic topology in like measure. The goal is a vibrational witnessing adequate to the deep structure of being in our era.

Poets participate in the planetary campaign when they become attuned to the endangered energies of earth, and let them shape the music of words. Both the energy and the endangerment have to enter the musical substratum of the poem. It's a matter of onto-acoustic realism.

◆

Thematically, *Testament* is bleak, with slivers of hope. Musically, it's bleak and hopeful at the same time.

The crunch is sonic, and the locus of hope is syllabic. There's a spirit of play at the heart of the linguistic mayhem, and if we listen kinesthetically to the destruction, we may also hear regeneration. The *no* and the *yes* at once.

◆

Being-at-all originated with the Big Bang. Ontogeny whoop-up. And some fractal of the original *yes* still resonates: that abruptly there *is* something, rather than nothing at all.

This white-hot miracle of being is where words have to start. Even if the miracle has become damaged goods on our watch. The poems suss out a fresh encounter with this blighted, pre-lingual immediacy. It's a high-risk zone, where language itself is at stake. But sometimes you have to stand as close to the flame as you can get. It's only then that the undermusic might begin to re-green.

And what comes next? Like you, I'm waiting to find out.

Coda

Sailaway Twain

Death closes all; but something ere the end,
Some work of noble note, may yet be done ...

Tennyson, "Ulysses"

I

You be the starlight, I'll be the Styx —
why not leave now?
Why dawdle our lives away?
It's time for one last run on parlous waters,
time to make the proverbs howl — here, at the
corner of Bloor & forever.
You be the carnival, I'll be the crunch —
why not leave now?

II

In my body, I first
drew breath. In my body
I sped through the seasons of human.
And in my body I will return to original dust.

For my mind still roams in the gravity fields of space-time —
but my body sags toward its patch of dirt.
And it tempts me to
leave what I love, and *hup* to the geezer brigade —
to gossip, infirmity updates,
and a dollop of whine.

It is
not who I mean to be, in my
final time.

III

I remember us in the story.
We were small, we were liminal, we were
known as the nesting nomads, the
sailaway twain. And always
amazed, my
edgy explorer — your mind like a greased neutrino,
high on the ozone hits. Now
daring yourself to go further / now

dormant in underthrum.
Witness to *juntas*. Witness to ambulant scum.
How can you be so beautiful, when you're so bereft?
Querida querido — wherever we
sail, stay
amazed.

IV

Meanwhile, back in the story,
a small boat bobs at the jetty, as if on
holidays.
The great lake echoes the blue. Across the harbour,
gulls opine.
You be the calculus, I'll be the cum —
Sailaway Twain, now playing.

For it's time to launch, to scud, to
shave the wind, as once the epic explorers and though our strength
is not our strength of old, old men can still dig
deep for the final departure and also to
put to sea in the Anthropocene is karmic
whiplash, we ply thru tech-
infested space the outbacks burning the very
sea we sail now septic and who,
who among humans
can re-green the earth, or tunnel an
exit to safety?

V

The waves bang harder now. Dusk thickens. The
wind begins to sting.
And into the garbage they go, the icecaps the wetlands the coral don't
get me started;
into the litter they skid it did
not have to be this way.

But our purpose holds: to
give true testimony —
time for one last run.
Two neophytes on earth, and now two
motes in the extinction cascade.
For I was born with a pang at the core, and always I hankered for
rhythms that matter.
And I remember babe I remember at night I
remember our deeds and our dreams, like an
ache in amber.
Sailaway twain.
You be the paradigm, I'll be the riffs —
that memory not go down
to the plenary dark.

2025

Acknowledgements

OVER THE DECADES, THESE ESSAYS HAVE BENEFITTED FROM exchanges with many colleagues and friends. I'm grateful to Donna Bennett, Robert Bringhurst, Russell Brown, Stan Dragland, George Grant, Sean Kane, Wendy Lesser, Don McKay, my wife Susan Perly, Zdravko Planinc, John Porter, Paul Vermeersch, Jan Zwicky.

My thanks to Anansi for hatching the parent collection, *Body Music*, in 1998.

Linda McKnight and Hilary McMahon, with their colleagues at the WCA agency, have been full-time angels since forever.

Natalya Rattan, of the Thomas Fisher Rare Book Library, helped me explore a wide range of material while I was writing the title essay.

Robert Bringhurst first wrangled the "Praise for Dennis Lee" and "Books by Dennis Lee" sections for *Heart Residence* (Anansi, 2017).

But this book's greatest debt is to George Galt, the editor at Stonehewer Books. His feel for how poems work, and his formidable B.S. detector, kept challenging me to find out what I actually think. Galt edits at an elite level.

And he was ably abetted by Ned Seager, whose crisp and empathetic copy-editing and imaginative design made this a better book.

My debt to Susan Perly, wordmate of forty years, is incalculable.

Notes on the Texts

ASIDE FROM "WRESTLING WITH CADENCE" AND "RE-GREENING the Undermusic," the essays here were selected from *Body Music* (Anansi, 1998). They have been variously shortened, lengthened, tweaked, revised, or totally reconceived. Credits and earlier publication details are as follows:

- In "Wrestling with Cadence," the descriptions of Osip Mandelstam's writing method come from *Hope Against Hope: A Memoir* by Nadezhda Mandelstam, translated from the Russian by Max Hayward. Copyright © 1970 by Atheneum Publishers (English Translation & Introduction). Reprinted with the permission of Scribner, an imprint of Simon & Schuster LLC. All rights reserved. The citations from James Gleick come from his biography *Genius: The Life and Science of Richard Feynman* (Pantheon Books, 1992).
- "Cadence, Country, Silence" began in 1972 as a ten-minute presentation at the third annual "Rencontre québécoise internationale des écrivains" in Montreal. An incomplete version was published in *Liberté*, 14, No. 6 (1972). It then appeared in *Open Letter*, Ser. 2, No. 6 (Fall 1973); *boundary 2*, 3, No. 1 (Fall 1974); and *The Threepenny Review*, No. 19 (Fall 1984).

- An early version of "Roots and Play" was delivered at the Loughborough International Seminar on Canadian children's literature, held in Toronto in 1975. It was published in *Canadian Children's Literature,* No. 4 (1976). Some of the poems here were written subsequently; all are now published by HarperCollins Canada.
- "Polyphony" began as an interview conducted by Jon Pearce in 1978. In rewritten form, it appeared as "Enacting a Meditation" in the *Journal of Canadian Poetry*, 2, No. 1 (Winter 1979). That led to the version published in the Lee issue of *Descant*, No. 39 (Winter 1982).
- "The Poetry of Al Purdy" appeared as the Afterword to *The Collected Poems of Al Purdy* (McClelland & Stewart, 1986). The poems here are quoted with the kind consent of Harbour Publishing. And the headnote comes from my introduction to *The Al Purdy A-Frame Anthology* (Harbour Publishing, 2009).
- "Memories of Miron" appeared in *Liberté*, 39, No. 5 (October 1997), in a translation by Marie-Andrée Lamontagne. The English original was published in *Brick, A Literary Journal*, No. 60 (Summer 1998).
- "The Luminous Tumult" is based on a 1993 interview conducted by Donna Bennett and Russell Brown. It appeared in *Poetry Canada Review*, 14, No. 2 (1994). And in 2015, it became the afterword in Brick Books' reissue of *Riffs*.
- "Poetry As a Mongrel Medium" is a reconsideration of the dialogue "Poetry and Unknowing." The latter drew on an interview by Michael Higgins, Peter Hinchcliffe, and John Porter, published in *The New Quarterly* (Summer 1994). It was then recast for *Poetry and Knowing* (Quarry, 1995), a volume of essays edited by Tim Lilburn.

- "Body Music" began as a background paper for a colloquium on "Dennis Lee and Canadian Literary Polyphony," held at Trent University in 1996. An expanded version appeared in *Thinking and Singing: Poetry and the Practice of Philosophy* (Cormorant, 2002), edited by Tim Lilburn. The present essay recasts the first half of that version. And in the headnote, "In Libya" comes from John Newlove's posthumous Selected, *A Long Continual Argument* (Chaudiere Books, 2007). Used by permission.
- "Re-Greening the Undermusic" began as the 2012 Ralph Gustafson Lecture at Vancouver Island University. It was published by Arbutus Editions in 2016, and is included here with the gracious consent of Joy Gugeler.

About the Author

Dennis Lee was born in 1939 in Toronto, where he has lived for most of his life. As an adolescent, he planned to become a professional magician. That changed, however, and he would go on to publish some forty books of poetry and prose.

Lee taught English literature at the University of Toronto until 1967, when he left to become a resource person at the experimental Rochdale College for two years and direct a small literary press, Anansi, till 1972. There he was part of a new literary ferment in English Canada. His landmark collection *Civil Elegies* appeared in 1968 and his children's classic *Alligator Pie* came out in 1974. He would continue to write poetry of both kinds to great acclaim.

From 1981 to 1984, Lee served as poetry editor at McClelland & Stewart. He also wrote most of the song lyrics for Jim Henson's television series *Fraggle Rock* (working with composer Phil Balsam) and contributed to the scripts of Henson's fantasy films *The Dark Crystal* and *Labyrinth*.

Lee was the first poet laureate of Toronto, serving from 2001 to 2004. During this time he started the Toronto Legacy Project, which marks the homes of notable figures in the city's history. And from 2011 to 2015 he was a resident artist at Soulpepper Theatre Company, where he initiated the "Lost Songs of Toronto" cabaret.

Heart Residence, Lee's Collected Poems, was published in 2017. He is married to the novelist Susan Perly and has three adult children and two grandchildren.